Letts
and
LONSDALE

ESSENTIALS

Year 8
KS3 English
Coursebook Answers

IMAGINATIVE WRITING

Page 7

Quick Test

1. The place or circumstance a story is set in.
2. Themes
3. Climax
4. First person; Third person

Page 8

Key Words Exercise

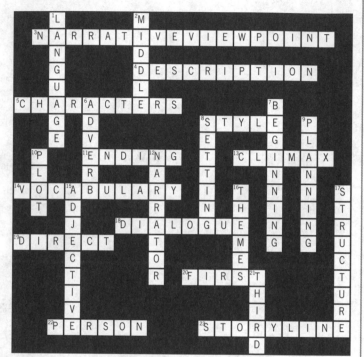

Page 9

Testing Understanding

1. The opening is important to capture the attention of the reader.
2. **Any three from:** An unexpected or unusual idea; By setting the scene; With dialogue that leads straight into the action; The description of a character; A dramatic event; By giving background information of the situation or characters
3. The way the story develops and the way the story is written.
4. So that the reader is left satisfied, perhaps with something to think about.
5. **Any two from:** A natural ending based on the development of the plot; A dramatic ending; An unexpected twist at the end; With information revealed that throws light on the characters or events; An ending that leaves things in the air and keeps you guessing
6. **a)** First **b)** First **c)** Third **d)** First **e)** Third
7. A word that describes a verb.
8. A word that describes a noun.
9. **a)** old (adjective); slowly (adverb); dusty (adjective)
   b) loudly (adverb); blue (adjective)
   c) slowly (adverb); golden (adjective); darkening (adjective)
   d) violently (adverb); trembling (adjective)
   e) quickly (adverb); smoking (adjective); suddenly (adverb)
10. There are too many adjectives used, which makes it sound flowery, exaggerated and artificial.

Page 10

Skills Practice

Make sure that you have carefully made notes on the stories and have covered the following points:
- How the writer sets the scene.
- If characters are introduced or described.
- If speech is used.
- What kind of opening each writer uses.

When writing your analysis, make sure that you use plenty of examples from your texts to support the points you make.

Extension Activity

Make sure that you include plenty of detail in your table. Use examples from the texts and explain how effective you think they are in engaging the reader.

CHARACTER AND ATMOSPHERE

Page 14

Quick Test

1. **a)** First person **b)** Third person
2. **a)** believable; convincing **b)** imagination

Page 15

Key Words Exercise

1. language 2. imagination 3. stereotypes 4. atmosphere / setting
5. mood / tone 6. adjectives 7. simile 8. metaphor 9. actions
10. feelings

Page 16

Testing Understanding

1. He was a **snub**-nosed flat-browed, common-faced boy enough; and as **dirty** a juvenile as one would wish to see; but he had about him all the airs and **manners** of a man. He was short of his age: with rather **bow**-legs, and little **sharp**, ugly eyes. His hat was stuck on the top of his head so **lightly** that it threatened to fall off every moment – and would have done so, very often, if the wearer had not had a knack of every now and then giving his head a sudden **twitch** which brought it back to its old place again. He wore a man's coat, which reached nearly to his heels. He had turned the **cuffs** back, half-way up his arm, to get his hands out of the sleeves: apparently with the ultimate view of **thrusting** them into the pockets of his corduroy **trousers**; for there he kept them.
2. An eerie or creepy atmosphere is created. Possible phrases that create the atmosphere include:
   - 'In the dusk.'
   - 'The rocket-hall was very dark.'
   - 'Footsteps sounded hollow.'
   - 'Bare boards.'
   - 'Intimate as a seaboot.'
   - 'Who could be listening?'

Page 17

Skills Practice

In creating your plan, think carefully about each stage. Include

Stage directions (getsa creditsoin) –   These tell you what's happening on stage.

Page 71

Testing Understanding

1. **a)** 'A Merry Christmas, Uncle! God save you!' cried a cheerful voice. It was the voice of Scrooge's nephew, who came upon him so quickly that this was the first intimation he had of his approach.
'Bah!' said Scrooge, 'Humbug!'
He had so heated himself with rapid walking in the fog and frost, this nephew of Scrooge's, that he was all in a glow; his face was ruddy and handsome; his eyes sparkled, and his breath smoked again.
'Christmas a humbug, uncle!' said Scrooge's nephew. 'You don't mean that, I am sure?'
'I do,' said Scrooge. 'Merry Christmas! What right have you to be merry? What reason have you to be merry? You're poor enough.'
'Come, then,' returned the nephew gaily. 'What right have you to be dismal? What reason have you to be morose? You're rich enough.'

    b) Here's one possible version. Yours may not be exactly like this because there is more than one way of putting it into indirect speech.
A cheerful voice had wished him a Merry Christmas and said that he wanted God to save him. It was Scrooge's nephew and he had come upon him so quickly that this had been the first intimation he had of his approach. Scrooge had dismissed this and said that he felt Christmas was humbug. Scrooge's nephew had heated himself with rapid walking in the fog and frost and was all in a glow, his face ruddy and handsome. His eye had sparkled and his breath was like smoke. He asked his uncle whether he really meant that Christmas was humbug and Scrooge had replied that he did. He went on to ask his nephew what right he had to be merry and what reason he had to be merry as he was poor. His nephew had answered gaily and had asked Scrooge what right he had to be dismal and morose as he was rich.

    c) Scrooge's nephew: (*cheerfully*) A Merry Christmas, Uncle!
    Scrooge: Bah! Humbug!

    (*Scrooge's nephew's face glowed and his eyes sparkled*)

    Scrooge's nephew: Christmas a humbug, uncle! You don't mean that, I am sure?

    Scrooge: I do. Merry Christmas! What right have you to be merry? What reason have you to be merry? You're poor enough.

    Scrooge's nephew: Come, then. What right have you to be dismal? What reason have you to be morose? You're rich enough.

Page 72

Skills Practice

You should have made sure when writing out the conversation you've recorded, that you use all the conventions of speech punctuation.

You should have paid particular attention to the use of...
*   layout and the correct placing of speech marks
*   the use of capital letters and of the use of other punctuation marks.
When converting this to indirect speech, you should have looked at...
*   the use of tense, pronouns and adverbs
*   the removal of speech marks.

Extension Activity

In creating your play script, you should have used...
*   the correct layout of speech and the correct tense
*   stage directions.

SPELLING

Page 76

Quick Test

1. Plurals 2. Sibilants 3. Homophones 4. Deer 5. Look it up in a dictionary

Page 77

Key Words Exercise

1.	accurate	8.	sound
2.	singular	9.	nouns
3.	consonants	10.	plurals
4.	collective	11.	meaning
5.	spelling	12.	dictionary
6.	homophones	13.	sibilance
7.	vowels		

Page 78

Testing Understanding

1. **a)** Classes **b)** Boxes **c)** Atlases **d)** Tables **e)** Windows **f)** Houses **g)** Inches **h)** Rays
2. **a)** boys **b)** qualities; opportunities **c)** mangoes; tomatoes **d)** heroes **e)** mosquitoes; weather **f)** trousers; waist; potatoes **g)** towed; buoys **h)** sopranos; haloes; lights
3. Todd and his **friends** followed the path into the valley. The **herds** of cattle roamed freely and there were lots of **sheep** too. All **manner** of **birds** flew in the sky and Todd and his **friends** felt the sun on **their** faces and the wind gently ruffle **their hair**. They had **heard** that **bears** roamed these hills but they didn't **see** any and so thought they must be in **their** lairs. In the streams they **saw** trout swimming and **salmon** jumping.

Page 79

Skills Practice

You should have identified the most common spelling mistakes and why the mistakes occur. Your poster should be clear and visually effective.

Extension Activity

In creating your PowerPoint presentation, make sure that your slides are clear. Present examples of wrongly spelt words and the corrected versions. Don't try to put too much information on one slide.

READING FOR MEANING

Page 83

Quick Test

1. Factual **2.** Style **3.** Analysing **4.** Point, Evidence, Explanation

Page 84

Key Words Exercise

1. Non-fiction **2.** Point, Evidence, Explanation **3.** Audience; Effect
4. Analysis **5.** Style **6.** Presented **7.** Topic **8.** Factual
9. Information **10.** Texts **11.** Ideas **12.** Illustrations **13.** Content

E	C	N	E	D	I	V	E	Z	S	F	L	A	U	N
Q	B	I	G	T	E	X	T	S	N	R	V	G	I	O
V	A	D	N	A	G	A	N	P	O	U	R	E	N	I
K	J	E	W	M	P	E	I	V	I	B	Q	S	N	T
P	B	A	E	P	J	F	A	C	T	U	A	L	O	A
C	D	S	S	T	Y	L	E	L	A	A	V	E	I	N
C	O	I	Z	U	L	F	Z	D	R	I	A	Z	T	A
L	T	N	V	S	F	B	R	E	T	H	N	L	C	L
C	B	N	T	E	K	P	Q	T	S	L	A	M	I	P
I	V	R	C	E	R	J	E	N	U	Q	L	T	F	X
P	H	T	I	A	N	W	S	E	L	I	Y	N	N	E
O	P	S	N	R	G	T	N	S	L	F	S	I	O	H
T	D	X	L	Y	Z	O	I	E	U	A	I	O	N	Y
A	U	D	I	E	N	C	E	R	E	R	S	P	R	T
A	S	R	M	D	O	E	A	P	T	O	P	C	S	N

Page 85

1. Testing Understanding

a) Audience: School children – the language suggests secondary age range. **Purpose**: To inform, advise and give help about being bullied. **b)** Tell someone. **c) Any three from:** Name calling; Making things up about someone so they get into trouble; Punching, hitting and physically hurting someone; Threatening someone; Taking someone's things off them; Spreading rumours about someone; Stealing from someone; Damaging someone's property; Sending threatening messages, e.g. e-mails, texts, etc. **d)** By suggesting they tell various people about it and different ways to tell them. **e)** The language is quite informal to make the reader feel at ease. It is straightforward vocabulary so it's easily understood. The tone is friendly and advising. **f)** Short paragraphs and bullet points help present the information clearly.

Page 86

Skills Practice

You should have chosen your piece of writing carefully and...
*   identified the audience and purpose
*   explained the key points the writer makes
*   examined carefully how the writer presents information
*   given examples of how language is used and the effects it creates
*   used the Point, Evidence, Explanation approach.

Extension Activity

Your discussion with a friend is an important element in this activity and you should have used the ideas from it as the basis for your review. Remember to think about the purpose and audience for your review when writing it.

ACKNOWLEDGEMENTS

The author and publisher are grateful to the copyright holders for permission to use quoted materials and images.

Every effort has been made to trace copyright holders and obtain their permission for the use of copyright material. The authors and publishers will gladly receive information enabling them to rectify any error or omission in subsequent editions. All facts are correct at time of going to press.

Letts and Lonsdale
4 Grosvenor Place
London SW1X 7DL

School orders:	015395 64910
School enquiries:	015395 65921
Parent and student enquiries:	015395 64913
Email:	enquiries@lettsandlonsdale.co.uk
Website:	www.lettsandlonsdale.com

ISBN: 978-1-906415-92-1

01/200309

Published by Letts and Lonsdale

© 2009 Letts and Lonsdale.

British Library Cataloguing in Publication Data.

A CIP record of this book is available from the British Library.

Book Concept and Development: Helen Jacobs
Commissioning Editor: Rebecca Skinner
Author: Steven Croft
Project Editor: Robert Dean
Cover Design: Angela English
Inside Concept Design: Helen Jacobs and Sarah Duxbury
Text Design and Layout: Ian Wrigley
Artwork: Letts and Lonsdale

Printed in Italy

Letts and Lonsdale make every effort to ensure that all paper used in our books is made from wood pulp obtained from well-managed forests, controlled sources and recycled wood or fibre.

Anagrams

1. Structure 2. Simile 3. Julius Caesar 4. Personification
5. Romances

Page 57

Testing Understanding

1. a) True b) False c) True d) True e) True f) False g) False
    h) False i) True j) False
2. a) Simile b) Simile c) Metaphor d) Metaphor e) Simile

Page 58

Skills Practice

Choose your soliloquies carefully and make sure that you have
explained…
*   where each soliloquy comes in the action of the play
*   who the speakers are
*   what ideas are contained in the soliloquies
*   what the soliloquies tell you about the characters
*   how the language is used (make sure you have given
    examples to support your points).

Extension Activity

Make sure that your information sheet is clear and explains the
differences between metaphors and similes effectively. It's a good
idea to think about the visual effects of the information sheet.

READING POETRY

Page 62

Quick Test

1. **Any three from:** Simile; Metaphor; Personification; Aural
    (alliteration, assonance, onomatopoeia)
2. Aural
3. Alliteration
4. Vowels
5. Onomatopoeia

Page 63

Key Words Exercise

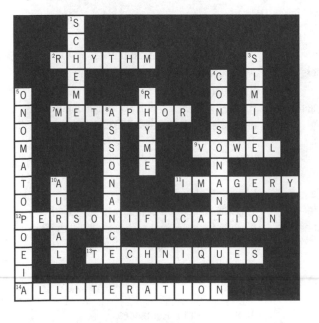

Page 64

Testing Understanding

1. a) Every footstep breaks a brittle pane; Dead boughs take roots
    in ponds; Ferns on windows shoot; Ranks trees in an armed
    host; Hangs daggers from house eaves b) Lurk under gluey
    glass like fish in bowls c) Tinkle d) Frost called to water; The
    sun will strike him dead e) AABBCC

Page 65

Skills Practice

Make sure that you have focused on the key areas suggested in the
activity. Remember – don't just identify features such as metaphors
and similes, but write about the effects that they create in the poem.

Extension Activity

You should have thought carefully about the questions for your
partner. Make sure that the questions are to do with how the
language is used rather than just what the poem's about.

PUNCTUATION

Page 69

Quick Test

1. Speech marks
2. When there's a new speaker
3. Past
4. Colon
5. Describe the actions or scenes and give instructions

Page 70

Key Words Exercise

Direct speech (credit cheeps) –	Speech that uses the exact words that are spoken.
Punctuation (auctionpunt) –	These marks help to make written English readable.
Indirect speech (crinedt secpeh) –	Speech that reports what's been said.
Reported speech (deporter hecspe) –	Another term for indirect speech.
Pronouns (snoopurn) –	Words that stand in place of the noun.
Tense (enset) –	Past and present are examples of this.
Present (restpen) –	The tense that describes things that are happening now.
Past tense (taps neets) –	This describes things that happened yesterday, for example.
Adverbs (verbsad) –	Words that tell you more about the verb.
Play script (layp prisct) –	A play is written in this.
Drama script (amard crispt) –	Another term for 'play script'.
Speech marks (peshce krams) –	These only go round the words that are spoken.
Quotation marks (tuqootain skarm) –	Another term for 'speech marks'.

enough detail to create a useful framework but avoid putting so much detail in that you're almost writing the story instead of a plan.

Extension Activity

When giving your talk make sure that you clearly explain...
- the decisions you made when planning your story
- the effects you wanted to achieve.

Be prepared to answer any questions they might have. Avoid writing out your talk and just reading it. Remember, this should be a talk and not just simply reading out your notes.

GRAMMAR

Page 20

Quick Test

1. True 2. False 3. False 4. False . False 6. True

Page 21

Key Words Exercise

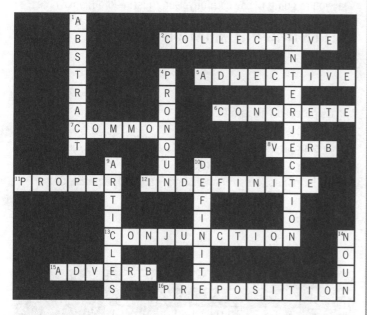

Page 22

Testing Understanding

1. Proper nouns – Harry; Mrs Tompkins
   Collective noun – Class
   Common nouns – Desk; Teacher; Essay
   Abstract nouns – Satisfaction; Fact; Excellence
2. a) pride b) poverty c) confidence
3. a) Pride b) Flock c) Team d) Shoal e) Herd f) Crew
   g) Regiment (or battalion, platoon) h) Colony (or army)
   i) Fleet or convoy j) Clutch k) Bouquet (or bunch) l) Pack
4. a) Her; It b) Its; She c) Their; They; Their
5. a) Last; Beautiful b) Grey; Bitter; Icy; Barren
6. a) Hard (describes work) b) Grimly (describes hung)
   c) Happily (describes smiled)
7. a) On (preposition); And (conjunction); Out of (prepositions)
   b) About (preposition); But (conjunction); Of (preposition)
   c) Out to (prepositions); And (conjunction); In (preposition);
      Of (preposition)
8. a) The (definite) b) A (indefinite) c) The (definite); An
   (indefinite)

Page 23

Skills Practice

Make sure that ...
- your poster is attractive and eye-catching
- your poster is simple to understand (avoid too much written explanation on it)
- you think carefully about how you lay out the information.

In designing your information leaflets, make sure that...
- each leaflet gives information about each word class
- you include examples to illustrate key ideas
- you present the information in an interesting way.

Extension Activity

Don't try to cram too much on each of your PowerPoint slides. Remember that you need to focus on the key ideas and try to make it as visually interesting as possible. Make sure your sound commentary is clear and fits your PowerPoint presentation.

AUDIENCE AND PURPOSE

Page 27

Quick Test

1. a) purpose b) complain c) inform d) people interested in birds or birdwatching
2. To instruct

Page 28

Key Words Exercise

1. Analyse 2. Complain 3. Entertain 4. Audience 5. Inform
6. Describe 7. Purpose 8. Argue 9. Persuade 10. Instruct
11. Advise 12. Explain

U	J	R	D	E	S	C	R	I	B	E	S	E	W
E	N	T	E	R	T	A	I	N	Y	W	S	E	H
C	C	O	M	P	L	A	I	N	D	O	W	D	Y
E	E	C	B	V	F	W	E	X	P	U	Q	A	H
Y	S	P	E	C	M	M	Q	R	O	D	Y	U	Y
C	Y	N	S	O	E	S	U	C	F	J	C	S	G
I	L	Y	I	E	O	P	K	I	Q	Z	B	R	Z
N	A	D	V	V	C	V	D	C	N	S	H	E	T
S	N	K	D	R	N	N	Z	Y	A	F	C	P	O
T	A	Q	A	M	T	Y	E	O	R	K	O	B	A
R	R	V	M	O	O	X	U	I	C	G	K	R	M
U	A	R	G	U	E	L	I	S	D	Y	L	T	M
C	A	O	H	C	M	L	N	M	F	U	H	E	T
T	S	G	B	R	X	C	E	X	P	L	A	I	N

Page 29

Testing Understanding

1. **Audience**: Readers who enjoy scary stories; **Purpose**: To entertain / describe (maybe also to inform)
2. **Audience**: Anyone interested in skateboarding; **Purpose**: To entertain / inform / advise
3. **Audience**: Someone cooking an Indian meal; **Purpose**: To instruct / inform / advise
4. **Audience**: Young children; **Purpose**: To entertain
5. **Audience**: Children of school age; **Purpose**: Maybe to inform / advise / persuade someone being bullied

6. **Audience**: Anyone reading about news items; **Purpose**: To inform
7. **Audience**: Young person at school studying science; **Purpose**: To inform / instruct
8. **Audience**: Someone who has sold a faulty camera; **Purpose**: To inform / persuade / complain
9. **Audience**: A young child; **Purpose**: To entertain
10. **Audience**: A young person at school or a teacher; **Purpose**: To analyse / inform / describe
11. **Audience**: Fans of *Doctor Who*; **Purpose**: To entertain / inform / describe
12. **Audience**: Someone with a headache; **Purpose**: To advise / inform
13. **Audience**: Someone who likes romantic stories; **Purpose**: To entertain / describe
14. **Audience**: Anyone planning to visit Paris; **Purpose**: To inform / advise

Page 30

Skills Practice

Choose your three pieces of writing carefully and make sure that for each one you...
* identify the audience and the purpose
* analyse the language (remember to use examples and comment on the effect they create)
* think about the presentation and the effect it has.

Extension Activity

Make sure you include some details of language use and presentation.

DEVELOPING A POINT OF VIEW

Page 34

Quick Test

1. False
2. False
3. True
4. True
5. True

Key Words Exercise

Page 35

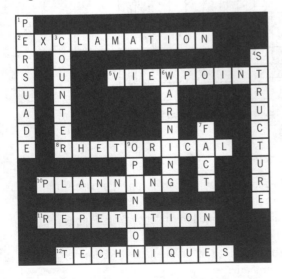

Page 36

Testing Understanding

1. Rhetorical question
2. Repetition
3. Outlining the problem / topic
4. Use of facts
5. Using views that don't agree with your own
6. Countering argument
7. Warning of consequences

Page 37

Skills Practice

Make sure that you choose your topic carefully and work through the steps, thinking clearly about each one. Check your rough draft carefully and make any changes that you think necessary.

Extension Activity

Make sure your talk does not last more than five minutes. Plan what you're going to say carefully. Don't just read out your notes.

PRESENTING INFORMATION

Page 41

Quick Test

1. Its purpose – to inform.
2. clear; easy to understand
3. To draw attention to certain points and present the ideas clearly.
4. Different styles of lettering.
5. Bullet points; Illustrations; Maps; Tables; Diagrams; Colour; Pictures; Photographs

Page 42

Key Words Exercise

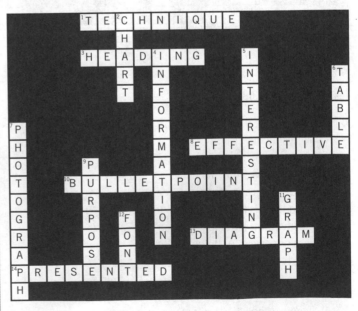

Page 43

Testing Understanding

1. Information is presented in a variety of ways:
   * Heading giving the name of the property and its location.
   * Written description.

- Photographs.
- A table giving dates and prices.
- Symbols to summarise key features and other information.

2. **a)** Eight **b)** Yes **c)** Yes **d)** No **e)** Yes **f)** £555 **g)** 4th July to 25th September at £785

Page 44

Skills Practice

Remember that the main purpose of your writing is to inform the reader. Make sure that your leaflet contains plenty of information that makes your chosen resort or town sound interesting.

Also, think carefully about layout. Don't try to cram too much into the leaflet.

Extension Activity

Think carefully about how could improve your leaflet in light of your partner's comments.

Use different fonts and colours on a computer to make the leaflet more effective.

MEDIA TEXTS – NEWSPAPERS

Page 48

Quick Test

1. Columns
2. Copy
3. Captions
4. Lead
5. Editorial

Page 49

Key Words Exercise

1. Headline
2. Tabloid
3. Broadsheet
4. Photographs
5. Report
6. Facts
7. News
8. Article
9. Reviews
10. Editorial
11. Advertisements
12. Copy
13. Caption
14. Journalist
15. Exclusive
16. Lead
17. Banner
18. Editor
19. Columns
20. Opinion

H	I	T	E	E	H	S	D	A	O	R	B	V
E	D	N	E	T	W	E	R	I	L	E	D	W
A	A	E	F	S	O	V	O	E	A	V	N	O
D	E	S	A	S	A	I	T	Y	D	I	O	R
L	L	I	C	N	R	S	I	I	V	E	I	P
I	A	U	T	M	T	U	D	T	E	W	T	H
N	E	W	S	U	I	L	E	S	R	S	N	O
E	D	T	U	L	C	C	O	I	T	D	O	T
R	I	H	A	O	L	X	N	L	I	I	I	O
H	T	O	P	C	E	E	O	A	S	O	N	G
V	O	Y	H	E	A	L	I	N	E	L	I	R
I	R	E	P	O	R	T	T	R	M	B	P	A
W	I	D	J	O	U	R	P	U	E	A	O	P
B	A	N	N	E	R	I	A	O	N	T	E	H
T	U	O	N	Y	E	E	C	U	T	A	D	S

Page 50

Testing Understanding

1. **a)** True **b)** False **c)** True **d)** False **e)** True **f)** True **g)** True **h)** False **i)** False **j)** True
2. **a)** Eye catching banner headline captures the attention.
   b) Sub-heading captures the drama of the event – note the alliteration of 'Rapid Response Rescue'.
   c) Opening paragraph sets the scene.
   d) Gives details of what happened – note the use of dramatic language. e.g. 'horrendous', 'huge', mountainous', and 'smashed'.
   e) Use of direct quotation.
   f) Use of expert opinion.
   g) Details about jet skiing adds background information.
   h) Reassuring conclusion ties up the details.

Page 51

Skills Practice

Make sure that you...
- choose the subject of your report carefully
- plan what you're going to put in it
- organise the structure
- word process it with a suitable eye-catching headline.

Extension Activity

1. Plan your questions carefully in advance but be prepared to take a different line or ask other questions if that seems a good idea.
2. Plan your report or article carefully, based on the information you've gathered.

SHAKESPEARE

Page 55

Quick Test

1. False 2. False 3. True 4. True 5. True

Page 56

Key Words Exercise

Simile –	A comparison, using the words 'like' or 'as'.
Plot –	The storyline of a play.
Histories –	Plays based on historical figures.
Metaphors –	A comparison, saying that one thing actually is the other.
Romances –	Plays that have a fantasy or magical element and were the last plays Shakespeare wrote.
Imagery –	The use of words to create a picture or 'image'.
Soliloquy –	What a character speaks while alone on stage.
Comedies –	Plays with a happy ending.
Structure –	The way the action of a play is put together.
Personification –	A kind of metaphor where something that's not human is described as if it has human feelings or qualities.
Tragedies –	Plays that end with the death of the main character(s).
Last plays –	Another term for Romances.

Steven Croft

ESSENTIALS

Year 8
KS3 English
Coursebook

How to Use this Coursebook

A Note to the Teacher

This coursebook includes coverage of the Level 1 Functional Skills for English appropriate to Year 8. Guidance and practice material relating to these skills is integrated into the main content of the book to reflect the structure of the new Programme of Study.

Each coursebook comprises...
- clear, concise content appropriate to that year
- questions and tasks to reinforce students' learning and help improve their confidence.

This coursebook is split into 12 topics. The first pages of a topic contain the content. They feature...
- **key words** picked out in colour in the text and listed in a box at the end of each topic
- a **Quick Test** to test understanding.

The final three pages in a topic contain questions and exercises to provide skills practice and reinforce students' understanding:
- **Key Words Exercise** – requires students to match the Key Words to their definitions.
- **Testing Understanding** – comprises a literacy exercise.
- **Skills Practice** – devoted to a relevant task to develop the students' English skills.

A pull-out answer book is included in the centre of this book. It contains the answers to the questions in the Quick Tests and to the practice sections of this coursebook.

Each coursebook is supported by a workbook for further practice and learning.

A Note to the Student

We're sure you'll enjoy using this coursebook, but follow these helpful hints to make the most of it:
- Make sure you understand the key words before moving on. These words include technical terms that you should be able to understand and use correctly, plus words that will help to expand and develop your vocabulary. If you don't understand them, look back at the context in which they're used to gain a sense of their meaning, ask your teacher or use a dictionary.
- Try to write in Standard English, use correct punctuation and good sentence construction. Read what you have written to make sure it makes sense. Some questions require extra research, using dictionaries, encyclopedias and thesauruses, or the internet.

- The tick boxes on the Contents page let you track your progress: put a tick in each box when you're confident that you know the topic.
- The questions marked with a light bulb symbol ( ) are included to help you focus on different aspects of the text. No answers are included. Instead, we suggest you write down your answers and discuss your ideas in pairs, in a small group or with your teacher.
- For many of the skills practice and extension questions, there is no right or wrong answer. Once you have your answer, refer back to the original question and make sure you have covered all the points, then ask a classmate or teacher to read your answer. Ask them questions to find out if you have communicated your ideas effectively.

Contents

Personal Writing

4   Imaginative Writing ☐
8   Key Words Exercise ☐
9   Testing Understanding ☐
10   Skills Practice ☐

Character and Atmosphere

11   Character and Atmosphere ☐
15   Key Words Exercise ☐
16   Testing Understanding ☐
17   Skills Practice ☐

Grammar

18   Grammar ☐
21   Key Words Exercise ☐
22   Testing Understanding ☐
23   Skills Practice ☐

Audience and Purpose

24   Audience and Purpose ☐
28   Key Words Exercise ☐
29   Testing Understanding ☐
30   Skills Practice ☐

Developing a Point of View

31   Developing a Point of View ☐
35   Key Words Exercise ☐
36   Testing Understanding ☐
37   Skills Practice ☐

Presenting Information

38   Presenting Information ☐
42   Key Words Exercise ☐
43   Testing Understanding ☐
44   Skills Practice ☐

Media Texts – Newspapers

45   Media Texts – Newspapers ☐
49   Key Words Exercise ☐
50   Testing Understanding ☐
51   Skills Practice ☐

Shakespeare

52   Shakespeare ☐
56   Key Words Exercise ☐
57   Testing Understanding ☐
58   Skills Practice ☐

Reading Poetry

59   Reading Poetry ☐
63   Key Words Exercise ☐
64   Testing Understanding ☐
65   Skills Practice ☐

Punctuation

66   Punctuation ☐
70   Key Words Exercise ☐
71   Testing Understanding ☐
72   Skills Practice ☐

Spelling

73   Spelling ☐
77   Key Words Exercise ☐
78   Testing Understanding ☐
79   Skills Practice ☐

Reading for Meaning

80   Reading for Meaning ☐
84   Key Words Exercise ☐
85   Testing Understanding ☐
86   Skills Practice ☐

88   Index and Acknowledgements

Imaginative Writing

What is Covered in this Topic?

This topic looks at...
- planning your story
- structuring your story
- first person and third person narratives
- ways to open and end your story.

Planning a Story

An interesting story that keeps the attention of the reader needs careful **planning**.

That's because many parts need to work together to create the overall effect of your story, which you need to think about before you start writing.

Plot, Structure

Story, Setting

Style, Language

Characters, Themes

Your story needs to have the following:
- **Plot** – what happens in your story (sometimes called the **storyline**).
- **Structure** – the order the events happen in your story and the way they link together; the way the story is built.
- **Characters** – the people (or animals, etc.) that you create and that your story centres around.
- **Setting** – the place, situation, circumstances, world, etc. that your story is set in.
- **Language** – the kinds of words (**vocabulary**) you use in your story.
- **Style** – the way in which you write your story.
- **Themes** – the ideas you put forward or draw attention to in your story (e.g. a story about someone being picked on at school might explore ideas about bullying).

Planning Your Approach

Here are two ways you can approach planning your story:

1. Think up your character or characters and create a story for them.
2. Think up your plot, then create your character(s) to fit in with the storyline.

Structuring a Story

In order to write an effective story, it's important to think about the structure and how the events that make up your plot will develop and link together.

When you plan your story you need to think about...

- the **beginning** – this needs to capture the reader's attention and make them want to read on
- the **middle** – in which you develop your plot, characters and ideas
- the **climax** – usually the story builds up to some kind of climax, key moment or event that leads to the ending
- the **ending** – this brings the story to some kind of conclusion.

The Beginning

You can begin a story in different ways. Here's how four different writers begin their stories.

💡 *What do you notice about how they begin?*

Captures the reader's attention with an unexpected idea.

> You can call me Link. It's not my name, but it's what I say when anybody asks, which isn't often. I'm invisible.
>
> *Stone Cold* by Robert Swindells

Begins with direct speech, which captures the reader's attention. The mention of a ghost arouses interest and makes the reader want to read on to find out what's happening.

> 'I can assure you,' said I, 'that it will take a very tangible ghost to frighten me.' And I stood up before the fire with my glass in my hand.
>
> 'It is your choosing,' said the man with the withered arm, and glanced at me askance.
>
> *The Red Room* by H.G. Wells

Describes and sets the scene.

> On the morning of the third day, the sea calmed. Even the most delicate passengers – those who had not been seen around the ship since sailing time - emerged from their cabins and crept on to the sun deck where the deck steward gave them chairs and tucked rugs around their legs and left them lying in rows, their faces upturned to the pale, almost heatless January sun.
>
> *Someone Like You* by Roald Dahl

Focuses on introducing and describing a character.

> When Farmer Oak smiled, the corners of his mouth spread till they were within an unimportant distance of his ears, his eyes reduced to mere chinks, and diverging wrinkles appeared round them, extending upon his countenance like the rays in a rudimentary sketch of the rising sun.
>
> *Far from the Madding Crowd* by Thomas Hardy

Imaginative Writing

Deciding How to Begin a Story

The important thing to do is capture your reader's interest at the beginning of the story. You could...

- begin with an unexpected and intriguing idea
- set the scene through vivid description
- begin with **dialogue** (**direct speech**) between your characters
- focus on a **description** of a character or characters
- give your reader information about the characters or situation
- begin with a dramatic event.

Developing Ideas

You need to plan the structure of your story carefully. Think about...

- how the events of your story unfold and link together
- how your characters develop and relate to one another
- creating a series of ideas to keep your reader interested and make them want to read on
- building up to some kind of climax or key moment in your story
- varying your use of language to keep your story interesting, lively and vivid.

Remember to...

- keep the action moving
- make your characters convincing – try to bring them to life
- use dialogue (speech) at various points to give added interest and make your story more interesting
- make your description vivid by using well-chosen **adverbs** (words that describe verbs) and **adjectives** (words that describe nouns), but don't overdo it or your writing will sound false and 'flowery'.

Points of View

Before beginning, you need to decide which point of view to use to tell your story. This is called the **narrative viewpoint**.

The two most commonly used points of view are **first person** narration and **third person** narration.

First and Third Person Narratives

In a first person narrative the **narrator** is actually a character in the story, so the 'I' narrator tells the story. This style of telling the story gives the feeling that the narrator is talking to you directly and tells everything from the point of view of the narrator character.

In third person narratives the narrator is outside the story and describes the characters and events as if they know everything that's going on. They can describe what's going on in the minds of all the characters and make comments on characters and events.

Third person

David woke up this morning

I woke up this morning

First person

Ending Your Story

Sometimes, story endings are disappointing. They can seem flat and lacking excitement or interest, or can just fizzle out leaving the reader thinking, 'So what?'

You should decide on the ending of your story as part of your planning. It's as important to think carefully about how to end your story as it is to think about how to begin it.

The ending should leave the reader feeling or thinking about something – they might feel satisfied, angry, puzzled, amused, intrigued, or any other emotion.

There are various ways to end your story. Here are some examples:
- End with a dramatic event.
- The story comes to a natural end based on the way the plot has developed.
- End by revealing some information or knowledge that throws light on the events or characters.
- An unexpected twist.
- An ending that leaves things up in the air and keeps the reader guessing or drawing their own conclusions – a cliffhanger.

Quick Test

1. What is meant by the 'setting' of a story?
2. What are the ideas explored in a story called?
3. What is the key event or high point of the story called (it usually comes towards the end)?
4. Give two types of narrative viewpoint.

KEY WORDS
Make sure you understand these words before moving on!
- Planning
- Plot
- Storyline
- Structure
- Character
- Setting
- Language
- Vocabulary
- Style
- Theme
- Beginning
- Middle
- Climax
- Ending
- Dialogue
- Direct speech
- Description
- Adverb
- Adjective
- Narrative viewpoint
- First person
- Third person
- Narrator

Imaginative Writing

Work out the key words from the clues below, then copy and complete the crossword.

ACROSS

3. The point of view a story is told from. (9, 9)
4. This allows the reader to imagine the scene or character. (11)
5. These live in your story. (10)
8. The way in which you write your story. (5)
11. The 'twist in the tale' is one kind of this. (6)
13. Key moment of a story. (6)
14. The words used in the story. (10)
18. Another word for speech. (8)
19. Type of speech, spoken. (6)
20. _____ person narrative uses 'I'. (5)
22. Stories are usually told in the first or third _____ narrative. (6)
23. Another name for the plot of a story. (9)

DOWN

1. The words you use to write your story. (8)
2. Part of story where characters are developed. (6)
6. A word that describes a verb. (6)
7. Opening to a story. (9)
8. Where the action of a story takes place. (7)
9. You need to do this before writing your story. (8)
10. Another word for storyline. (4)
12. They tell the story. (8)
15. A word that describes a noun. (9)
16. The ideas you explore in your story. (6)
17. The way that events of the plot link together. (9)
21. In a _____ person narrative the narrator is not a character in the story. (5)

Testing Understanding

1 Why is the opening of a story important?

2 Give three ways in which you could begin a story.

3 What is the structure of a story?

4 Why is the ending of a story important?

5 Give two ways in which you could end a story.

6 Read the following sentences and identify whether they're written in the first person or in the third person.
   a) I turned slowly to look at Zoe and felt that our efforts had been worthwhile.
   b) My uncle was the strangest man I had ever known, but he thought that I was the odd one.
   c) Sam thought she would never finish her story – she just could not think of an ending she was happy with.
   d) We seemed to have been waiting for hours but Jim said that we had only been there for fifteen minutes.
   e) She opened the door carefully, feeling very frightened about what she might find.

7 What is an adverb?

8 What is an adjective?

9 Read the following sentences and identify the adverbs and adjectives.
   a) The old man hobbled slowly up the dusty road.
   b) 'Not that one!' shouted Kim loudly. 'You need the blue folder.'
   c) The sun slipped slowly below the skyline, leaving only a golden glow in the darkening sky.
   d) The wind blew violently and the rain rattled against the trembling windows.
   e) He leapt quickly out of the way as the smoking car veered suddenly off the road and mounted the pavement.

10 What do you think is wrong with the following paragraph?

> The deep, rich blue of the bright, clear, sparkling summer sky with its fluffy, delicate cotton-wool white clouds added to the calm, beauty and tranquillity of the lovely, peaceful scene. The golden, warming, smiling sun shone down on the green, gold-spattered, empty fields.

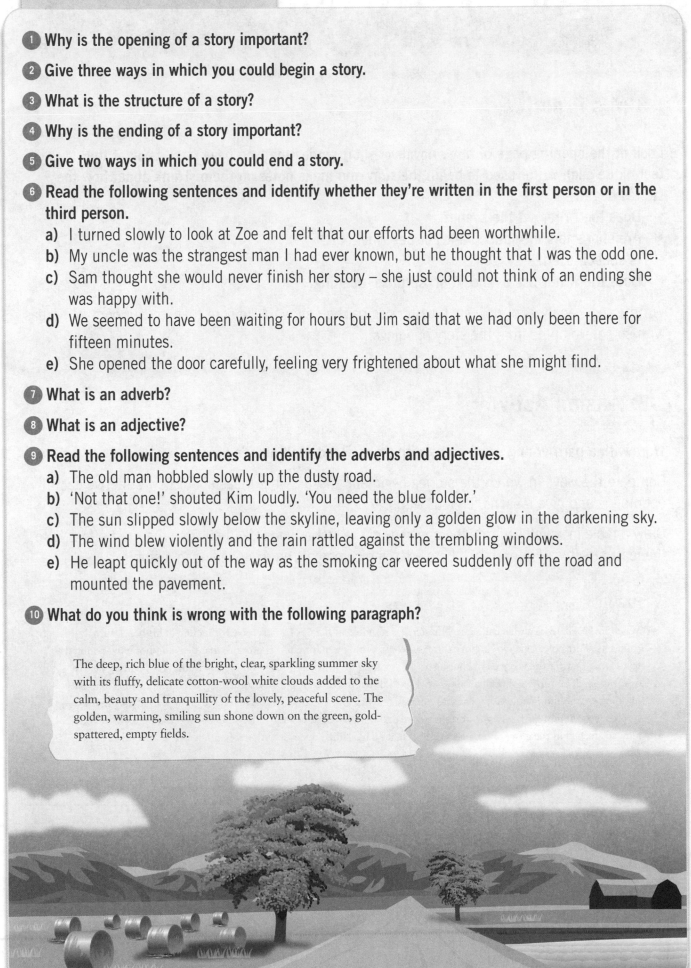

Imaginative Writing

Look at the opening page of three novels or short stories that you have read. Look at the technique each writer used to begin the story and make notes on them. Think about how the stories begin:

- **Does the writer set the scene?**
- **Are characters introduced and / or described?**
- **Is speech used?**
- **Does the writer use a 'shock' or 'surprise' opening?**

Write a short analysis of how each writer begins their story. Make sure that you support your ideas with some examples from the story openings.

Extension Activity

Work with a partner and swap notes with them. Read each other's notes.

Compare the ways in which the stories begin and discuss your ideas about how effective each opening is and give reasons for your views.

Draw a table in which you rate the openings of the stories you looked at, from the most effective to the least effective. For example, here are some comments on this opening to a story:

> 'Halloa! Below there!'
>
> When he heard a voice thus calling to him, he was standing at the door of his box, with a flag in his hand, furled round its short pole. One would have thought, considering the nature of the ground, that he could not have doubted from what quarter the voice came; but instead of looking up to where I stood on the top of the steep cutting nearly over his head, he turned himself about, and looked down the Line. There was something remarkable in his manner of doing so, though I could not have said for my life what. But I know it was remarkable enough to attract my notice, even though his figure was foreshortened and shadowed, down in the deep trench, and mine was high above him, so steeped in the glow of an angry sunset, that I had shaded my eyes with my hand before I saw him at all.
>
> *The Signalman* by Charles Dickens

Novel or Short Story	How it Opens	Comments
The Signalman by Charles Dickens	Direct speech (someone shouting), then a description of how the man acts and a description of the scene.	The opening exclamation, 'Halloa! Below there!', immediately captures the reader's attention. The man acts strangely, which makes the reader want to read on and find out why. The 'angry sunset' creates an ominous note.

Character and Atmosphere

What is Covered in this Topic?

This topic looks at...
- using language effectively
- creating convincing characters
- setting the scene
- creating atmosphere.

Creating Characters

Characters are a very important part of a story and they come in all shapes and sizes. They may not even be human – in some stories the characters are animals or aliens from space.

The characters you create for your stories are made up from your **imagination**. Sometimes, though, writers create new characters using ideas from their own experiences and people they have met.

Creating Believable Characters

The key points to remember when creating characters are to...
- avoid **stereotypes** (unconvincing 'cardboard cut-out' characters)
- make them believable and convincing.

The table contains some techniques and ideas you could include in your story.

convincing

believable

Technique	Ideas
Description	• Give some information about your characters. • Describe how they look. • Give ideas about their attitudes and **feelings**. • Describe their **actions**.
Dialogue	• What the characters say and how they speak tells the reader a lot about them. • What other characters say about them can be revealing.
Thoughts and feelings	• Letting the reader know what's going on in a character's mind.
Actions	• How the character behaves and reacts to other characters.

Character and Atmosphere

Introducing Characters

In the following two passages the writers use two different approaches to introducing characters.

💡 *What do you notice about them?*

Nightmare Stairs by Robert Swindells

She's Mum's big sister, Auntie Anne, but they're not a bit alike. Or if they are I can't see it. Mum's nice, you know? A really nice person – the sort who'll go out of her way to do someone a good turn, even a complete stranger. Auntie Anne isn't. No way. I'll tell you the sort of person she is. Suppose she's in the car park and it's Saturday afternoon and the place is full, right? She's loaded her shopping into the boot and she's ready to leave when she notices someone waiting for her space. Instead of starting up and pulling away like she meant to, she'll find a cloth and get out and start working her way round the car, really slowly, doing the windows and mirrors. They don't need doing – she's making the guy wait, that's all. And if he gives up and moves on she's really glad. I know she's my auntie but I've no time for her. In fact I hate her and I always have.

The Secret Passage by Nina Bawden

When John and Mary and Ben Mallory first saw their Aunt Mabel they thought she looked very disagreeable. She was tall and thin with a long, thin face and grey hair insecurely fastened in a straggly bun at the back of her neck. Whenever she turned her head, a little shower of hairpins fell out. When she met the children at London Airport, she was wearing a faded brown coat and stockings that wrinkled on her skinny legs as if they had been intended for a much fatter person.

John thought she probably looked like that, so shabby and cross, because she was a widow. His father had told him that her husband, Mr Haggard, had been drowned at sea.

In *Nightmare Stairs* the writer...
- uses first person narration
- uses a comparison between her mother and Auntie Anne to tell us straightaway that her auntie isn't a nice person – a detailed example of her auntie's behaviour is given to illustrate this.

In *The Secret Passage* the writer ...
- uses third person narration
- gives the names of the characters
- describes what Aunt Mabel looks like
- gives an idea of what John thinks about her.

Settings

The **setting** is an important part of your story. You need to think carefully about how you're going to describe it. Here's an example of a writer describing a setting.

💡 *How does the writer create an impression of the setting?*

The Lord of the Flies by William Golding

The shore was fledged with palm trees. These stood or leaned or reclined against the light and their green feathers were a hundred feet up in the air. The ground beneath them was a bank covered with coarse grass, torn everywhere by the upheavals of fallen trees, scattered with decaying coco-nuts and palm saplings. Behind this was the darkness of the forest proper and the open space of the scar. Ralph stood, one hand against a grey trunk, and screwed up his eyes against the shimmering water. Out there, perhaps a mile away, the white surf flinked on a coral reef, and beyond that the open sea was dark blue. Within the irregular arc of coral the lagoon was still as a mountain lake – blue of all shades and shadowy green and purple.

The writer uses several techniques in the extract:

- The use of **adjectives**, such as *green* feathers, *coarse* grass, *fallen* trees and *decaying* coco-nuts.
- The use of **metaphors** – the shore was 'fledged' with palm trees (fledged is a word used to describe a young bird with feathers that's ready to leave the nest) and the trees' leaves are described as 'green feathers'.
- The use of a **simile** – 'still as a mountain lake'.
- He describes the setting as it is seen through the character Ralph's eyes.

💡 *How many more adjectives can you spot?*

Adding Detail

When writing your own story you can help your reader to 'see' the setting in their mind by...

- adding small touches of detail as you develop your story
- using longer passages (as in the example above) in which you give a more detailed description of the setting.

Character and Atmosphere

Atmosphere

The **atmosphere** of a piece of writing is closely linked to the **mood** or **tone** created. Words that might come into your mind when you think about atmosphere could include these: peaceful, friendly, happy, tense, frightening, spooky, exciting, sad, edgy, creepy.

Creating an Atmosphere

Atmosphere is the special feeling created by a writer's description of the action or setting in a story. It creates the mood of the writing or the feelings created in the reader's mind.

💡 *How would you describe the atmosphere created in this extract from* Dracula *by Bram Stoker?*

> Soon we were hemmed in with trees, which in places arched right over the roadway till we passed as through a tunnel; and again frowning rocks guarded us boldly on either side. Though we were in shelter, we could hear the rising wind, for it moaned and whistled through the rocks, and the branches of the trees crashed together as we swept along. It grew colder and colder still, and fine, powdery snow began to fall, so that soon we and all around us were covered with a white blanket. The keen wind still carried the howling of the dogs, though this grew fainter as we went on our way. The baying of the wolves sounded nearer and nearer, as though they were closing round on us from every side.

The passage creates a feeling of tension or fear, which the writer creates through his use of the **language** or vocabulary. For example...

- 'hemmed in with trees' creates the sense of being in a tunnel
- 'frowning rocks' creates a threatening feeling
- 'the rising wind' and 'moaned and whistled' add to the creepy atmosphere
- 'It grew colder and colder' adds to the tense atmosphere
- 'the howling of the dogs' and 'the baying of the wolves' creates an eerie and ominous sound effect.

Quick Test

1. What kind of narration is used in each of these sentences?
   a) My name is Joe and I'm thirteen years old.
   b) The boy's name is Joe and he is thirteen years old.
2. Complete the following sentences:
   a) You should try to make your characters _____ and _____ .
   b) In creating your characters you need to use your _____ .

KEY WORDS
Make sure you understand these words before moving on!
- Imagination
- Stereotype
- Feeling
- Action
- Setting
- Adjective
- Metaphor
- Simile
- Atmosphere
- Mood
- Tone
- Language

Key Word Exercise

Complete each sentence by finding the missing key word.

1 In order to create a convincing picture of your characters you need to use

_____ effectively.

2 You use your _____ to create your characters.

3 Making your characters convincing will prevent them being _____, or

'cardboard cut-outs'.

4 You might create an eerie _____ when writing a ghost story.

5 Atmosphere in writing is closely connected to _____ .

6 _____ can make your description more vivid by telling you more about

the nouns in your writing.

7 Another useful way of making your description more vivid is by using a

_____ to compare the thing you're describing to something else.

8 A _____ is like a simile but doesn't use 'like' or 'as'.

9 The things that characters do are called their _____ .

10 You can describe what characters think about other characters and events, which reveals

their thoughts and _____ .

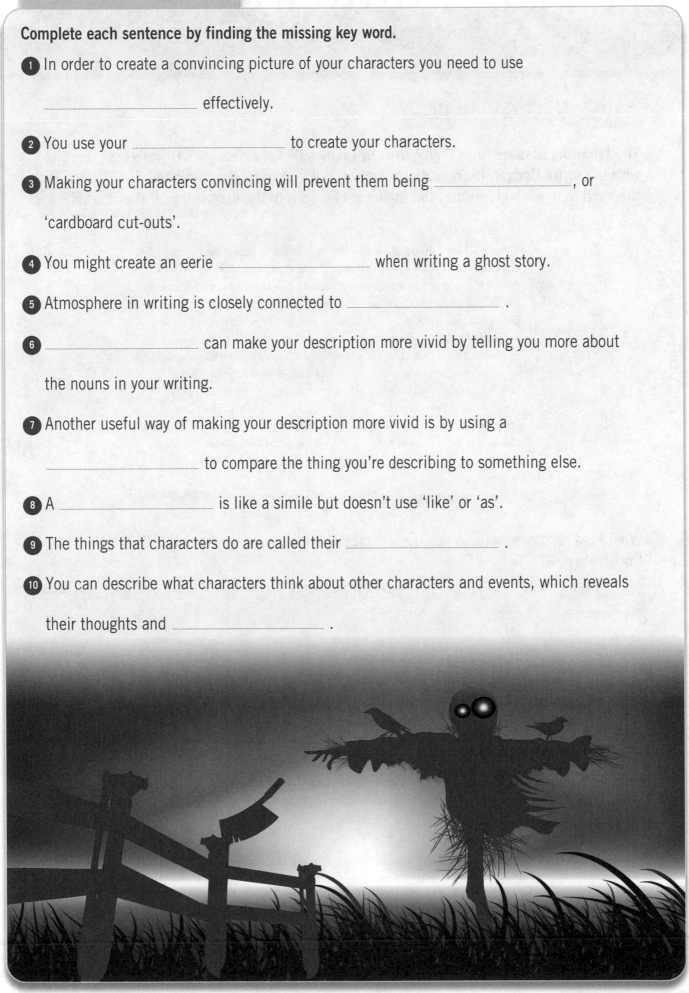

Imaginative Writing

1 The following passage from *Oliver Twist* by Charles Dickens describes Oliver's first meeting with the Artful Dodger. Dickens concentrates on the physical description of The Dodger. Pick the word from each group that you think best fits in with the description of the character.

> He was a **bent / snub / sharp**-nosed, flat-browed, common-faced boy enough; and as **dirty / small / strange** a juvenile as one would wish to see; but he had about him all the airs and **tricks / ideas / manners** of a man. He was short of his age: with rather **round / bow / barrel**-legs, and little, **glassy / sharp / tired**, ugly eyes. His hat was stuck on the top of his head so **firmly / lightly / tightly**, that it threatened to fall off every moment – and would have done so, very often, if the wearer had not had a knack of every now and then giving his head a sudden **twitch / nod / shake** which brought it back to its old place again. He wore a man's coat, which reached nearly to his heels. He had turned the **material / cuffs / lapels** back, half-way up his arm, to get his hands out of the sleeves: apparently with the ultimate view of **pushing / thrusting / placing** them into the pockets of his corduroy **trousers / shirt / vest**; for there he kept them.

2 What kind of atmosphere do you think is created in this passage from *The Watch House* by Robert Westall?

Write down any word or phrase that you think helps to create this atmosphere and explain your choices.

> As they reached the door, Anne gave one last look back. In the dusk at the far end of the room, Arthur's model lighthouse had begun flashing at last.
>
> 'Run back an' switch it off – there's a good lass. Then turn the key in the lock an' fetch it when ye come.' Arthur started towards the cottage, whistling.
>
> Anne suddenly wished Arthur had waited. The rocket-hall was very dark, now the lights were off. She hurried down it with her eyes on the floor. Her footsteps sounded hollow on the bare boards. Hollow, and too loud in that private place. But who could be listening?
>
> She pushed the switch over, and the lighthouse stopped flashing. As she turned back, she made the mistake of looking up. All around her, the twisted dusty blackened gear of foreign dead men hung. Too much of it. Personal, intimate as a sea-boot, and old.

Skills Practice

Plan the first stages of a story of your own.

Stage 1: Decide on the type of story you're going to write, e.g. an adventure story, a ghost story, a school story, etc.

Stage 2: Decide on your narrative viewpoint.

Stage 3: Write down the key points of your plot (don't have too many – try to summarise it in a maximum of 10 points).

Stage 4: Structure the events of your story, expanding a little on the key points of your plot. Remember that you will need...
- an effective opening to capture the interest of your reader
- interesting events that keep your reader's interest and build up to a climax or key moment
- an effective ending (think carefully about the effect you want to achieve at the end).

Stage 5: Make a list of your characters and make notes on them. Remember:
- Don't have too many characters. In a short story you don't have the space to develop too many characters. It's better to have a small number of well-developed, convincing characters.
- Give your characters individual characteristics or features to make them more interesting and convincing.

Stage 6: Decide on the setting or settings of your story. Think carefully about how you're going to present it. Remember to describe your setting effectively to help make your story convincing and interesting to read.

Extension Activity

After you've planned your story, prepare a short talk to give to a small group of friends or students in your class. In your talk you should...
- **explain the decision you made when planning your story**
- **explain the effects that you want to achieve**
- **answer any questions that they might have.**

You should try to be as clear as possible when presenting your ideas to the group.

ideas

Friends lost
haunted house
no electricity

Grammar

What is Covered in this Topic?

This topic looks at...
- word classes
- written forms of language.

Word Classes

The term 'word classes' is the name given to the basic types of words that the English language is made up of.

It will help you to use English correctly if you can identify the different kinds of words you use when writing and understand what they do.

Word Classes	What it Does
Noun	Nouns name things, such as people, places, things, and ideas.
Pronoun	Used instead of a noun (for example, 'he', 'she').
Verb	Describes some kind of action (it's sometimes called a 'doing word').
Adjective	A word that describes a noun.
Adverb	A word that describes a verb.
Conjunction	Joins two words or parts of a sentence together (it's sometimes called a 'joining word' or connective).
Preposition	Usually used with nouns or pronouns and shows a connection between the noun or pronoun and the rest of the sentence, e.g. The man put his book on the table – *on* tells you where he put the book.
Interjection	A word that expresses emotion or surprise (for example, 'Ouch!', 'Hurry!').
Article	Used to introduce a noun (for example, 'the', 'a', 'an').

Word Classes in Action

Here are all the word classes working together in a sentence:

Noun → **Tom** | Verb → **ran** | Adverb → **quickly** | Preposition → **to** | Article → **the** | Adjective → **corner** | Noun → **shop** | Conjunction → **but** | Pronoun → **it** | Verb → **was** | Adjective → **closed**, | Interjection → **oh no!**

Tom ran quickly to the corner shop but it was closed, oh no!

Nouns and Pronouns

There are different kinds of nouns:
- **Common nouns**: these name general everyday things and objects around us (for example, 'table', 'car', 'dog', 'river', 'computer', 'sky').
- **Concrete nouns**: a kind of common noun which describes something physical that you can see, hear, smell, taste or feel (for example, 'pen', 'chair', 'water').
- **Abstract nouns**: things we can't see or touch, like feelings and emotions (for example, 'love', 'fear', 'pride', 'confidence', 'generosity').
- **Proper nouns**: the names of specific people, places, times, events, books, etc. (for example, 'Sandra', 'York', 'Tuesday', 'the Great Fire of London', 'River Thames', '*Great Expectations*').
- **Collective nouns**: the names of groups or collections of things (for example, 'a herd of cows', 'a flock of birds', 'a swarm of bees').

Pronouns take the place of a noun in a sentence. They can save a lot of repetition of nouns (for example, 'I', 'he', 'she', 'they', 'it', 'me', 'you', 'us', 'them').

Verbs

Verbs are one of the most important parts of speech. It's not possible to have a sentence without a verb. In fact, a verb can make a sentence all on its own, for example, 'Run!'; 'Stop!'; 'Go!'; 'Jump!'; 'Sit!'

Verbs are doing words – they describe actions, such as 'Jane *kicked* the ball'. They are *being* words and describe states such as, 'The radiator *was* very hot', or 'Your dog *seems* friendly'.

Adjectives and Adverbs

Adjectives tell you more about (or describe) the nouns or pronouns. They usually come in front of the noun or pronoun, for example...
- the *blue* boat ploughed through the *heavy* sea
- the *tall*, *powerful* man had *short*, *cropped* hair.

Adverbs tell you more about verbs – they tell you where, how or when something was done. For example...
- the burglary happened *here*
- he looked at me *angrily*
- you shouted at me *yesterday*.

Grammar

Conjunctions

Conjunctions (or connectives) join parts of a sentence together, as in the following examples:

- 'He jumped for the ball. He missed it.' becomes 'He jumped for the ball *but* he missed it.'
- 'Do you want an ice-cream? Do you want a lollipop?' becomes 'Do you want an ice-cream *or* do you want a lollipop?'

Commonly used conjunctions:

- And
- But
- Or
- Although
- As
- That
- If.

...although

Prepositions & Interjections

Prepositions show the relationships between two parts of a sentence. For example…

- he sat *on* the sofa
- you can't leave the classroom *without* permission
- we stayed *near* Scarborough
- the text message was *from* David.

Interjections are exclamations, short phrases or single words that express feelings such as surprise, shock, disgust and anger. For example…

- Ah! Ow! Yippee!
- Hooray! Phew! Ouch!

Articles

Articles come before a noun. There are three words that are normally called 'articles':

- 'A' and 'an' are **indefinite** articles.
- 'The' is the **definite** article.

Note the difference that the use of an indefinite or a definite article can make:

- *The* car broke *a* speed limit as it tore down *the* road.
- *A* car broke *the* speed limit as it tore down *a* road.

Quick Test

1. True or false – an adjective tells you more about a noun.
2. True or false – Manchester is a common noun.
3. True or false – an interjection joins two parts of a sentence together.
4. True or false – a pronoun can replace an adjective.
5. True or false – 'run' is a preposition.
6. True or false – 'a', 'an' and 'the' are articles.

KEY WORDS

Make sure you understand these words before moving on!

- Noun
- Pronoun
- Verb
- Adjective
- Adverb
- Conjunction
- Preposition
- Interjection
- Article
- Common noun
- Concrete noun
- Abstract noun
- Proper noun
- Collective noun
- Indefinite
- Definite

Work out the key words from the clues below, then copy and complete the crossword.

Across

2. 'Flock' and 'herd' are examples of this kind of noun. (10)

5. A word that describes a noun. (9)

6. 'Table' is an example of this type of noun. (8)

7. This type of noun describes an everyday object. (6)

8. 'Run' is an example of one of these. (4)

11. 'John' and 'River Avon' are examples of this type of noun. (6)

12. 'A' and 'an' are this kind of article. (10)

13. Joins two parts of a sentence together. (11)

15. A word that describes a verb. (6)

16. 'On', 'in', and 'at' are examples of this. (11)

Down

1. 'Pride' and 'kindness' are this kind of noun. (8)

3. Ouch! is an example of one of these. (12)

4. 'Him', 'her', 'we', and 'them' are examples of this. (7)

9. 'The', 'a', and 'an'. (8)

10. 'The' is called the _____ article. (8)

14. A word that names something. (4)

Grammar

1 **Find the nouns in the following passage and identify what kind of noun each one is.**

Harry walked back to his class and sat down at his desk. He felt great satisfaction in the fact that the teacher, Mrs Tompkins, had praised the excellence of his essay.

2 **Form abstract nouns from the following words in brackets.**

a) Sean's face beamed with (proud) _____ when he received the prize.

b) In Dickens' time many people lived in (poor) _____ .

c) Rachel showed a lot of (confident) _____ before taking her driving test.

3 **Give the collective nouns for the following words.**

a) Lions   b) Sheep   c) Footballers   d) Fish   e) Cows   f) Sailors

g) Soldiers   h) Ants   i) Ships   j) Eggs   k) Flowers   l) Wolves

4 **Identify the pronouns in the following sentences.**

a) Kate worked hard on her story and had finished it before the end of the day.

b) The horse reared up on its hind legs and threw the rider, but luckily she was unhurt.

c) The family packed their belongings, even though they were unsure about moving to their new home.

5 **Identify the adjectives in the following sentences.**

a) We went on holiday last week and the weather was beautiful.

b) The grey sky looked threatening as the bitter, icy wind blew hard across the barren landscape.

6 **Find the adverbs in the following sentences and say which verbs they describe.**

a) I will work hard to pass my exams.

b) Todd grimly hung on to the rope.

c) Kim smiled happily at the news.

7 **Which words are conjunctions and which are prepositions in the following sentences?**

a) The boy slammed his book on the desk and walked out of the room.

b) I tried to write a story about the weather but I couldn't think of any ideas.

c) Billy went out to the field and joined in a game of football.

8 **Identify the definite and indefinite articles in the following sentences.**

a) This is the book I told you about.

b) I had a lovely sleep.

c) The teacher ate an apple.

Skills Practice

Working with a partner, design a poster for the wall of your classroom, explaining the basic word classes.

You should…
- make your poster eye-catching
- keep it simple – don't try to explain too much, but give the basic explanation of each word class
- think carefully about the layout.

Now design a series of information leaflets to accompany your poster:
- Each leaflet should give information about each word class.
- Include examples to illustrate the key ideas.
- Present the information in an interesting way.

Extension Activity

With your partner, prepare a presentation designed to teach the key ideas of word classes.

You could use PowerPoint or slides to illustrate the presentation.

Record a sound commentary to go with your presentation.

VERB (doing word)

NOUN (naming word)

Example:

Tom ran quickly

Audience and Purpose

This topic looks at…
- different kinds of purpose
- different kinds of audience
- writing to inform and instruct
- writing for an audience.

Purpose

It's important to recognise that every piece of writing that's produced has a **purpose** and is aimed at a particular **audience**.

The purpose of a piece of writing can vary tremendously – it can range from describing complex ideas on a topic to a scribbled note asking for a parcel to be left next door.

No matter how important or how trivial the writing is or seems, it's likely to have a purpose.

Here are some broad purposes that writing can have (sometimes a piece of writing might have more than one of these purposes):

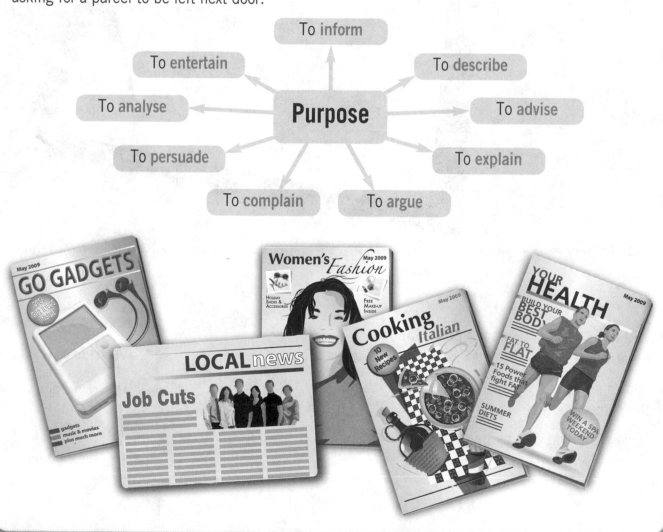

To inform

To entertain

To describe

To analyse

Purpose

To advise

To persuade

To explain

To complain

To argue

Audience

The audience that a piece of writing is aimed at can be as varied as its purpose. The audience could be...

- very broad (e.g. everyone), *or*
- very narrow (one person).

Your writing could be aimed at a particular audience, for example...

- people of a particular age group or gender
- people who do a particular job
- people who share an interest
- an individual person.

How many more types of audience can you think of?

Deciding on Your Audience and Purpose

Although purpose and audience are different things, the two are very closely linked. To decide on the audience and purpose of a piece of writing, you should...

- ask yourself why the piece was written – the answer to that question will tell you the purpose
- ask yourself who the piece is aimed at – the answer to that question will tell you the audience.

Writing to Inform an Individual

Here is a note you might write for your milkman.

The note was written to inform that you only want two pints of milk. It was written for the milkman.

2 pints today please

So, a note to your milkman will have an audience of one person – the milkman – and its purpose will be to inform him of how much milk you want.

Audience and Purpose

Writing to Inform Many People

A national newspaper report might have the same purpose as a milkman's note – to inform – but its audience could be millions of people.

BLIZZARDS BLAST BRITAIN

Yesterday most parts of the country were blasted by gale force winds and blinding blizzards as temperatures plummeted to well below freezing.

Writing to Instruct

A recipe could have the purpose to **instruct** you how to make a particular dish. Its audience might be anyone who's interested in making that dish.

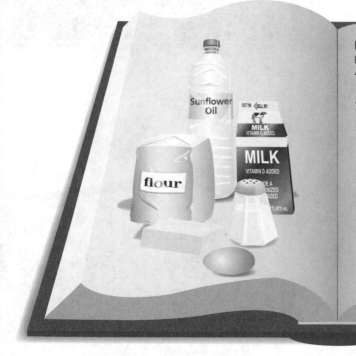

How to Make Yorkshire Pudding
Ingredients
4oz (100g) plain flour
1 medium-sized egg
A pinch of salt
½ pint (280ml) of milk (or mixture of milk and water)
2oz (50g) lard / fat or 2 tablespoons of oil –
sunflower oil is a healthier option.

Instructions
Mix the flour and salt in a basin and make a hollow in the middle.
Drop the egg into the hollow and stir in with a wooden spoon.
Add the milk gradually, stirring all the time until the flour is worked in.
Pour the mixture into a muffin tray and cook in the oven for 25 minutes.

Writing for a Particular Audience

A child's nursery rhyme is written for a particular audience. It could have the purpose to entertain and the audience would be young children, such as the following example:

> Hickory, dickory, dock,
> The mouse ran up the clock.
> The clock struck one,
> The mouse ran down,
> Hickory, dickory, dock.

Particular Audiences

The table shows some examples of purposes for writing and the audiences they're aimed at.

💡 *Think about other types of writing and their audiences and purposes.*

Type of Writing	Audience	Purpose
Website giving information on 'cheats' or 'walkthroughs' on a computer game.	Anyone interested in learning more about that computer game.	To inform the audience about ways to get through different levels of the game.
A story from a bedtime story book.	A young child.	To entertain and help them go to sleep.

Quick Test

1. Complete the following sentences:
   a) The _____ is the reason why a piece of writing is written.
   b) If you're not satisfied with something, you might write to _____ .
   c) The purpose of a newspaper is to _____ .
   d) The audience of an identification book on British birds would be _____ .
2. What would be the purpose of a leaflet on how to mend a puncture?

Audience and Purpose

Work out the key words from the clues below, then find them in the word search.

U	J	R	D	E	S	C	R	I	B	E	S	E	W
E	N	T	E	R	T	A	I	N	Y	W	S	E	H
C	C	O	M	P	L	A	I	N	D	O	W	D	Y
E	E	C	B	V	F	W	E	X	P	U	Q	A	H
Y	S	P	E	C	M	M	Q	R	O	D	Y	U	Y
C	Y	N	S	O	E	S	U	C	F	J	C	S	G
I	L	Y	I	E	O	P	K	I	Q	Z	B	R	Z
N	A	D	V	V	C	V	D	C	N	S	H	E	T
S	N	K	D	R	N	N	Z	Y	A	F	C	P	O
T	A	Q	A	M	T	Y	E	O	R	K	O	B	A
R	R	V	M	O	O	X	U	I	C	G	K	R	M
U	A	R	G	U	E	L	I	S	D	Y	L	T	M
C	A	O	H	C	M	L	N	M	F	U	H	E	T
T	S	G	B	R	X	C	E	X	P	L	A	I	N

1 To examine ideas or language carefully.

2 You might do this if you're not happy.

3 Novels and short stories might do this.

4 All writing aims at one of these.

5 Newspapers _____ readers.

6 Writing that gives you a clear picture of a scene could _____ it.

7 Asking yourself why a piece of writing has been written will tell you its _____ .

8 You might do this if you don't agree with someone else's view.

9 You might do this if you want to change someone's mind.

10 A set of instructions for setting up a new computer does this.

11 A leaflet telling you about smoke detectors in the home will _____ you about them.

12 Instructions can help to _____ how to do something.

Testing Understanding

Give your ideas on the audience and purpose of the following types of writing.

The audience and purpose of each type of writing might not always be clear-cut, but write down your ideas, giving various possibilities.

1. A ghost story.
2. A magazine article on skateboarding.
3. A recipe for onion bhajis.
4. A fairy tale.
5. A '*Kidscape*' web page on school bullying.
6. A newspaper report about a freak snowstorm.
7. A chapter in a text book on Science for lower secondary pupils.
8. A letter of complaint about a faulty camera you bought from eBay.
9. A bedtime story.
10. A homework essay on a Shakespeare play.
11. A '*Doctor Who*' story.
12. The leaflet in a packet of headache tablets.
13. A romantic novel.
14. A guide book on Paris.

Audience and Purpose

Find three different kinds of writing that you come across in everyday life.

You could choose some of the following types:

- A leaflet
- A newspaper report
- Instructions
- A letter
- An advertisement
- An extract from a text book
- An encyclopaedia entry
- The opening of a novel
- A poem
- A review.

Look carefully at the three pieces of writing that you've chosen. For each one...

- identify the audience
- identify the purpose
- analyse how each one uses language – pick out individual words and phrases and say what effects you think they give
- say what effects the layout or presentation has.

MP3 PLAYER QUICK-START INSTRUCTIONS

1. Turn the unit on by pressing the red button on the top of the player.
2. Set the player to "Audio" or "Video" mode by moving the slider on the side to the desired position.
3. If you wish to play an audio or video track, then press the button marked
4. If you wish to pause a track, then press
   [Note – this will drain the battery more quickly than with normal use]
5. If you wish to skip or browse through tracks, then press
   [Note – there is no facility to scan through audio files. In "Video" mode, simply keep the button pressed to scan through the file]
6. Volume is controlled by the dial at the side.
7. To turn off the unit, simply press the red button again.

ON/OFF
PLAY
STOP
PAUSE
SKIP
AUDIO/VIDEO
BATTERY

Extension Activity

Work with a partner and compare the pieces you selected and what you found.

Talk about your findings. Make a chart of your results on a large sheet of paper. You could lay it out like this:

Type of Writing	Purpose	Audience	Language Used	Presentation or Layout

Developing a Point of View

What is Covered in this Topic?

This topic looks at...
- the ways that views can be presented
- writing persuasively.

Presenting a Point of View

Some kinds of writing involve presenting a point of view on a particular topic or issue. Often the point of this writing is to argue a case or **persuade** the reader to take a particular **viewpoint**.

The following piece of writing gives an argument in favour of wind farms. Look carefully at how the writer puts forward her point of view.

Don't Let the Lights Go Out

Do you want to stop climate change? Do you want to use clean, renewable energy that will not harm the environment? If the answer to these questions is YES then you must support the development of wind energy. These farms could provide us and future generations with an energy source that will not run out.

Once the wind farms have been built they provide a clean, renewable source of energy with no pollution or waste products to deal with.

Another point in their favour is that they occupy such a small amount of land. They can be placed on farmland and the farmers can still farm the land around them. If they are no longer required in a certain area they can be dismantled and removed and the environment will not have been harmed.

Some people say they are an eyesore and ruin the landscape, but if they are carefully sited their visual impact can be lessened. On the other hand, some people feel that wind farms are not ugly and don't spoil the views. In contrast they think they look impressive and do not detract from the beauty of the countryside at all. Wind farms can also be built offshore where there is plenty of wind and where they are not even visible from the shore.

If we are to save our environment and keep the lights on, we must act now, otherwise it will be too late. Support wind farms!

Developing a Point of View

Techniques to Add Effect

The use of **rhetorical questions** and **repetition** can add effect to a sentence.

Rhetorical questions...
- are questions that aren't meant to be answered
- are meant to give the impression that the answer is obvious
- are used to add effect and emphasise a viewpoint to writing or speech.

Repetition is used in the wind farm extract to add emphasis to the point, for example, 'Do you want...?', 'Do you want...?'

This repetition makes it clear that the sensible answer must be yes. It's meant to encourage the reader to agree with the writer's views.

By using these techniques, the writer's viewpoint is developed, with points made in favour of wind farms.

Counter Arguments

A **counter argument** is when you take the opposite view of an argument and give points to counter those views.

Here are some useful words and phrases when countering a view that doesn't agree with your own:
- But
- Nevertheless
- Alternatively
- On the other hand
- Some people feel / think
- The most important thing is.

Emphasis

A **warning** of effects or consequences can add emphasis to a piece of writing. For example, the sentence, 'If we are to save our environment and keep the lights on, we must act now otherwise it will be too late' is saying that if you don't do something soon, something will happen that can't be stopped.

The use of **exclamations** adds emphasis to the points made, such as 'Support wind farms!', and creates the impression that the writer is passionate about their views.

Fact and Opinion

When views are expressed on a topic you will probably find that those views contain both **fact** and **opinion**.

💡 *Have another look at the piece on wind farms. Can you see both fact and opinion in it?*

The table shows some of the facts and opinions that you might have noticed in the wind farm article.

Facts	• Wind farms don't pollute the atmosphere or produce waste products. • Wind farms occupy a relatively small land area. • Wind farms can be taken down. • Wind farms can be built out at sea.
Opinions	• Wind farms are an eyesore. • Wind farms ruin the landscape. • Wind farms look impressive. • Wind farms don't spoil the beauty of the countryside.

Expressing Your Own Views

When writing a piece in which you express your own views on a topic, it's important that you plan carefully.

You could use the following approach when **planning** your piece:

1 Think carefully about the topic you're going to write about and make sure that you're clear in your mind about it.

2 Decide on your point of view.

3 Write down all the ideas you can think of both *for* and *against* the view you've taken.

4 Decide on the points you're going to make.

5 Arrange your points in a logical order that develops your ideas clearly.

6 Think about the evidence you'll use to support your views.

7 Decide how you're going to end your piece of writing.

Developing a Point of View

Structuring Your Writing

You can now plan the **structure** of your writing:

1. Introduction – an opening paragraph in which you catch your reader's attention and make the topic clear. It should also explain your basic point of view.
2. Main section – presents the points in favour of the view you're taking, giving reasons and evidence to support it. You could also include points that don't agree with your view and counter them.
3. Conclusion – briefly sums up your ideas and emphasises your point of view. You need to think of a way to create some kind of impact at the end that leaves your reader thinking.

Use different **techniques** to make your points, for example…

- rhetorical questions
- repetition
- counter arguments
- warnings
- exclamations.

Don't over-use any of these techniques, especially exclamations, rhetorical questions and repetition – they'll lose their impact if you use them too much.

Remember that you need to…

- create an impact in your opening
- express your views clearly
- structure your ideas logically
- support your points with evidence
- use other viewpoints and counter them
- have a strong conclusion.

Wind farms

Eyesore?
Impressive?

FACTS – Don't pollute
         – No waste

Quick Test

1. True or false – an opinion is definitely true.
2. True or false – a rhetorical question requires an answer.
3. True or false – writing needs careful planning.
4. True or false – an exclamation can add emphasis.
5. True or false – if you use any one technique too much it can lose its effect.

KEY WORDS
Make sure you understand these words before moving on!

- Persuade
- Viewpoint
- Rhetorical question
- Repetition
- Counter argument
- Warning
- Exclamation
- Fact
- Opinion
- Planning
- Structure
- Techniques

Key Words Exercise

Work out the key words from the clues below, then complete the crossword.

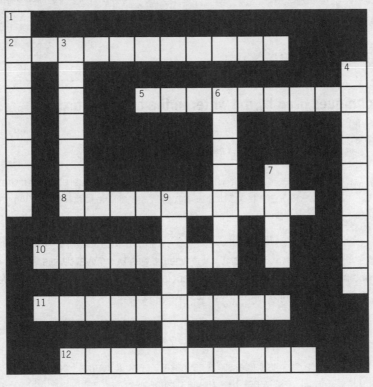

Across

2. You shouldn't use these too much! (11)
5. A way of looking at things. (9)
8. Don't bother answering this question. (10)
10. A good piece of writing requires thinking ahead. (8)
11. A technique that can be used to emphasise a point. (10)
12. You might use a variety of these to make your writing more effective. (10)

Down

1. Give a point of view to influence the reader. (8)
3. You might give this kind of argument when you don't agree with someone's point of view. (7)
4. To present your views effectively you need to arrange them in an order. (9)
6. Take notice of this if you know what's good for you. (7)
7. No question about this. (4)
9. This might be true – or maybe not. (7)

Developing a Point of View

Identify the seven techniques used by the writer in the following text.

NOWHERE TO GO

① Have you ever felt like an outcast? That's what it's like to be a skateboarder these days. We just have nowhere to go. It's as simple as that. Nowhere to go. Why is that? Well your guess is as good as mine. **②**

③ We used to skate in the town centre using the steps by the Town Hall and the ramps in the car park. Of course, we didn't try it when it was busy. We always waited until the shops had closed and it was quiet. If people were around, we moved on. We don't go out of our way to annoy people. We just want to skate.

The trouble is, we have nowhere to go. The council has banned us from skating in the town centre but have not provided us with any facilities.

There have been proposals to create a new skate park at Tunnet Park but it has been reported in the local newspaper that these proposals have been turned down and this has been confirmed by Councillor Lamber. This was because of the number of objections from people. Some people seem to feel that skateboarders are hooligans **⑤** out to cause trouble. On the other hand, all the evidence from areas where skate parks have been built shows that young people who use the skate parks don't cause any trouble and no longer try to skate in the town. **⑥**

Another argument that some people use is that the skate park would take up a huge part of the park. In fact, the plans show that the skating ramps would occupy an area of 60m long by 40m wide, with the highest ramp being 5m high. This is a very small part of the park, which is a mile long and nearly a mile wide. **④**

⑦ The nearest skate park is almost 30 miles away and that is too far to use on a regular basis. Other facilities are poor too. The nearest swimming pool is twenty miles away. There is one playing field and very few clubs for young people to go to. If young people in our town are not provided with better facilities then we are likely to see more young people hanging around street corners with nothing to do. Is this what we want? The answer has got to be – No! No! No!

Skills Practice

Choose a topic that you feel strongly about and prepare your ideas, ready to write a persuasive essay on it.

Step 1: Choose your topic. Make sure you choose a topic that you have views about.

Step 2: Make sure you're clear what your views on the topic are.

Step 3: Write down all your ideas on the topic. It's useful to make a list of all the points both *for* and *against* the view you've taken. You might want to use some of the arguments against your view to counter them.

Step 4: Decide on the key points that you're going to make and what evidence you're going to use to support them.

Step 5: Structure your ideas in a logical order.

Step 6: Think about how you're going to finish your piece of writing. Remember that you should try to leave your reader thinking about the points you've raised.

Step 7: Write a rough draft of your essay and then check through it carefully.

Step 8: Make any changes you think necessary to improve it further and do a final draft.

Extension Activity

Using the ideas from the essay you wrote, prepare a talk on the topic. Your talk shouldn't last more than five minutes.

When preparing your talk...
- **decide how much information you're going to include**
- **write a list of the points that you're going to make.**

You might find it helpful to prepare some small cards with short words or phrases on to prompt your memory and make sure that you don't miss anything out.

Don't...
- write out your speech in full
- try to learn your speech as it'll sound unnatural when you give it
- try to read out your speech because then it's more like reading out an essay – using only prompt cards will help you to resist the temptation to rely on notes.

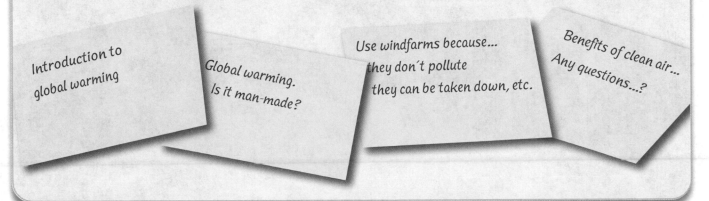

Presenting Information

What is Covered in This Topic?

This topic looks at...
- different forms of information
- different techniques for presenting information.

Information

Information comes in many different forms and can be **presented** in lots of different ways.

The diagram shows some forms of information that you might have noticed before.

Although these are very different kinds of writing, they have one thing in common – their **purpose**.

Their purpose is to inform the reader in one way or another. They may have other purposes too, but to inform the reader is a key one.

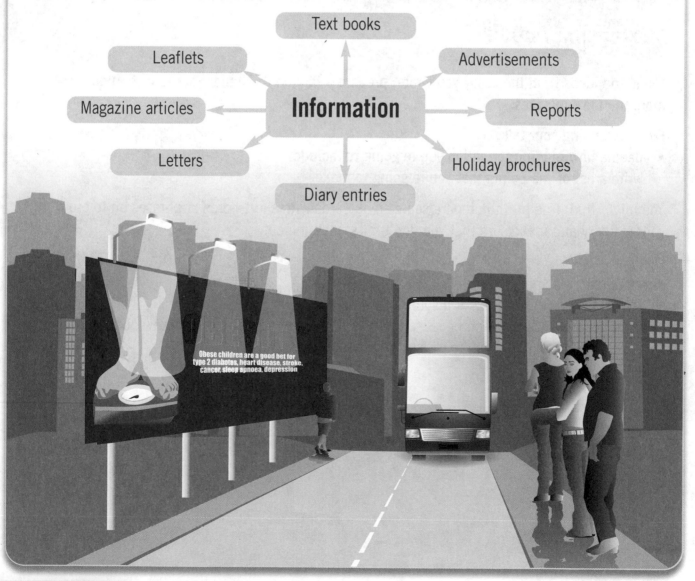

Text books

Leaflets

Advertisements

Magazine articles

Information

Reports

Letters

Holiday brochures

Diary entries

Obese children are a good bet for type 2 diabetes, heart disease, stroke, cancer, sleep apnoea, depression

Presenting Information Techniques

Information presented in texts should be clear and easy to understand.

Various **techniques** can be used to present information in an **interesting** and **effective** way.

There are many typical features that you might find used when presenting information.

Headings

Sub-headings

Bullet points

Different **fonts**

Different sizes of letters

Use of colour

Bold print

Underlining

Diagrams

Photographs

Graphs and **charts**

Tables

THIS IS A HEADING
This is the sub-heading of this poster

It includes:
- bullet points
- bullet points
- bullet points

Also **different** fonts *USED* in text

Different sizes of
letters used

Use of colour within text

Words stand out using **BOLD** text or by <u>underlining</u>

Also use tables, charts and graphs

Facts	• Wind farms don't pollute the atmosphere or produce waste products. • Wind farms occupy a relatively small land area.
Opinions	• Wind farms are an eyesore. • Wind farms ruin the landscape. • Wind farms look impressive. • Wind farms don't spoil the beauty of the countryside.

$y = x^2 - x - 6$

Presenting Information

Look at the following leaflet to see how information is presented.

How many features of presenting information can you spot in this leaflet? Think about the effects they create.

EXCITING INDOOR AND OUTDOOR FUN POOLS

The Waterland

Fun for all the family

Open daily from 9am to 6pm

The Waterland, Padstow, Cornwall
Information Hotline: 01232 23435
email: waterland@yahu.com

THERE'S LOADS TO DO...

Relax and swim in our Large Indoor Fun Pools and our superb Outdoor Pool. A tropical adventure pool for the whole family.

WHATEVER YOUR AGE
WHATEVER THE WEATHER

- Fabulous Water Flumes
- Stunning River Rapids Ride
- Water Cannon, Geyser, Fountains, Waterfall
- Toddlers' area and slide
- Cafe, craft shop and souvenirs

COME AND JOIN US FOR THE DAY

WE ARE HERE — Padstow — Bodmin — Newquay — A39

PRICES for 2009 season

	Off-peak	Peak (Jun 20-Sept 5)
Adults	£4.00	£5.00
Children (5-14yrs)	£2.50	£3.00
Under 5s	FREE	FREE
Family Pass (2 adults, 3 children)	£13.50	£15.50

Special rates for birthday parties and group bookings. Phone for details.

Identifying Techniques (cont.)

A range of techniques are used to make the holiday leaflet interesting, easy to read and full of detailed information.

The leaflet uses some of the following techniques:
- Large letters draw attention to key messages, for example, 'Loads to do' and 'Exciting indoor and outdoor fun pools'.
- Use of sub-headings.
- Use of bullet points to list special attractions.
- Language to attract the reader, for example, 'relax', large', 'superb'.
- The idea that the weather conditions don't matter.
- Details of prices.
- Eye-catching illustrations.
- Use of colour.
- Opening times are given.
- Map to show location.
- Further details, for example, telephone number, e-mail address, web address.

Quick Test

1. What does all writing that presents information have in common?
2. Complete the following sentence: When you're presenting information in writing, it should be _____ and
   _____ .
3. Why would you use bullet points in a piece of writing?
4. What are fonts?
5. What techniques other than writing could you use to present information?

KEY WORDS
Make sure you understand these words before moving on!
- Information
- Presented
- Purpose
- Technique
- Interesting
- Effective
- Heading
- Bullet point
- Font
- Diagram
- Photograph
- Graph
- Chart
- Table

Presenting Information

Key Words Exercise

Unscramble the anagrams to find the key words, then copy and complete the crossword.

Across

1. Quenchite
3. Ahendig
8. Fevetfice
10. Tublel toinp (2 words)
13. Raidgam
14. Spendtree

Down

2. Thrac
4. Monitorfain
5. Tennistiger
6. Taleb
7. Ghothoprap
9. Sorepup
11. Pargh
12. Tonf

Carefully read the following holiday brochure and look at the kind of information that it contains.

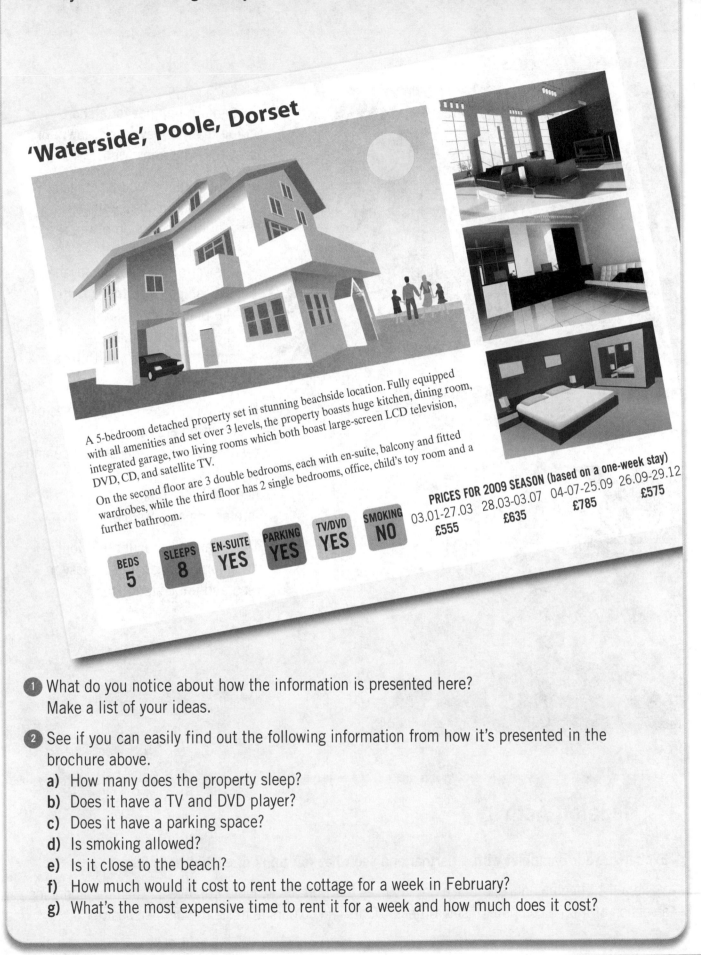

'Waterside', Poole, Dorset

A 5-bedroom detached property set in stunning beachside location. Fully equipped with all amenities and set over 3 levels, the property boasts huge kitchen, dining room, integrated garage, two living rooms which both boast large-screen LCD television, DVD, CD, and satellite TV.

On the second floor are 3 double bedrooms, each with en-suite, balcony and fitted wardrobes, while the third floor has 2 single bedrooms, office, child's toy room and a further bathroom.

BEDS	SLEEPS	EN-SUITE	PARKING	TV/DVD	SMOKING
5	8	YES	YES	YES	NO

PRICES FOR 2009 SEASON (based on a one-week stay)

03.01-27.03	28.03-03.07	04-07-25.09	26.09-29.12
£555	£635	£785	£575

1 What do you notice about how the information is presented here? Make a list of your ideas.

2 See if you can easily find out the following information from how it's presented in the brochure above.
   a) How many does the property sleep?
   b) Does it have a TV and DVD player?
   c) Does it have a parking space?
   d) Is smoking allowed?
   e) Is it close to the beach?
   f) How much would it cost to rent the cottage for a week in February?
   g) What's the most expensive time to rent it for a week and how much does it cost?

Presenting Information

Design a pamphlet for a short guide to a holiday resort, town, or area that you know well.

Your pamphlet should contain...
* a title and sub-headings
* a brief description of the resort, town or area
* the various attractions available
* the things to do there
* the places to see
* the location or map
* any other things you think are important.

Remember – the main purposes of your writing are to inform the reader about your chosen place and to persuade them to visit, so you need to try to make it sound as interesting as possible.

Think carefully about the layout – the information should be easy to read and understand.

Extension Activity

Exchange your pamphlet with a partner and see what you think of each other's ideas.

Make a list of comments and make any changes that you think would improve it. Then try producing a version of it on a computer, using different fonts and colours to make it more persuasive.

Media Texts – Newspapers

What is Covered in this Topic?

This topic looks at…
- different types of newspapers
- the content of newspapers
- features of newspaper articles
- analysing a newspaper article.

Newspapers

All newspapers **report** news in some way but not all newspapers are the same. They can be very different in…
- the kind of **news** they cover
- the ways in which they cover the news
- the range of other material they contain
- their size
  - large format newspapers (e.g. *The Daily Telegraph*) are **broadsheets**
  - smaller format newspapers (e.g. *The Mirror*, *The Sun*) are **tabloids**.

Types of Newspapers

💡 *Think about the different newspapers that you've seen and write them down.*

Type of Newspaper	What it Covers
National daily paper	Usually reports national and international news.
Regional daily paper	Covers the daily news of a particular town or area.
Weekend paper	Most national daily papers produce special editions on Saturdays and Sundays. These present news but often include items and free magazines covering various areas such as leisure, fashion, reviews, etc.
Weekly paper	Produced one day a week and usually covers a particular town or area.
Free paper	Normally based in one area; contains some news but has a lot of advertisements.

Media Texts – Newspapers

Contents of a Newspaper

Newspapers typically contain the following content:

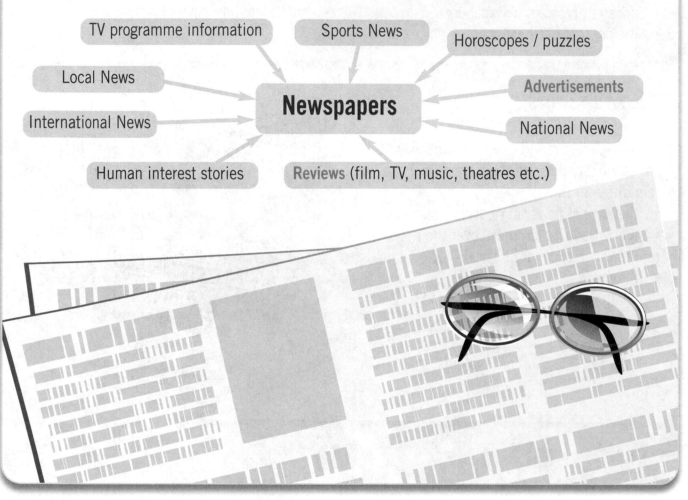

TV programme information

Sports News

Horoscopes / puzzles

Local News

Newspapers

Advertisements

International News

National News

Human interest stories

Reviews (film, TV, music, theatres etc.)

Features of a Newspaper

Newspapers are presented in a particular way:
- Stories and **articles** have **headlines** – the big headline on the front page is called a **banner**.
- The main story (also called the **lead story**) is on the front page and sometimes continues inside the newspaper.
- Newspapers often present a view on the main stories in a separate column called an **editorial**. The **editor** decides which stories and reports are to be included.

- Newspaper reports contain a lot of **facts**, although they sometimes contain **opinion** as well.
- Sometimes only one newspaper has the details of a particular story – this is called an **exclusive**.
- The text (or **copy**) is written in **columns** – the stories and reports are written by **journalists**.
- Pictures or **photographs** are often used, which usually have a title or explanation called a **caption**.

Weekly NEWS

Along Came a Spider!

The Golden Orb Weaver spider: caught on camera attacking a bird.

A giant spider has been caught on camera eating a bird in Australia.

A Chestnut-breasted Mannikin was the unlucky victim, flying into the web of a Golden Orb Weaver spider and becoming trapped.

Although you might expect this kind of thing to happen every day in wild jungles and far-off places, this took place in somebody's back garden.

Steve Johnson, an expert in spiders, said, 'The Golden Orb Weaver spider spins very strong and large webs. Birds are part of their diet.'

After the bird flew into the web in Cairns, Australia, it became exhausted. When the bird became weak, the spider attacked. It then used its poison to break down the bird, ready to eat.

Golden Orb Weaver spiders are found in warm countries such as Australia, Africa and parts of the USA.

Luckily for us, a bite from one of these would feel like a sting and wouldn't kill you.

---

1. Striking headline taken from *Little Miss Muffet* nursery rhyme.
2. Opening paragraph introduces topic of spider and sets the scene – Australia.
3. Use of actual names of species involved.
4. Shock effect of this happening in a back garden.
5. Quotation on the strength of the spider's web from an expert with personal experience.
6. Further details of what happened and where.
7. Details of where these spiders are found.
8. Reassuring final line.
9. Caption on photograph helps explain what is happening.

Media Texts – Newspapers

💡 *Try writing an analysis of the article about the spider.*

To help you, here are some points to think about:

- How the headline catches the attention.
- How the opening paragraph is effective.
- How the use of the actual names of the bird and spider add effect.
- How the information that this happened in a back garden makes you feel.
- How the use of direct speech from the expert adds effect.
- How the details of how the spider dealt with the bird adds interest.
- How the final paragraph is effective.
- The effect of the article on the reader.
- The use of quotations.

Quick Test

1. How is the text of newspapers laid out?
2. What is the written material that reporters provide called?
3. What do photographs and pictures normally have alongside them?
4. What is the main story of a newspaper called?
5. Complete the following sentence:
   The column in which a view is expressed about the main story is called an
   _____ .

KEY WORDS
Make sure you understand these words before moving on!

- Report
- News
- Broadsheet
- Tabloid
- Review
- Advertisement
- Article
- Headline
- Banner
- Lead
- Editorial
- Editor
- Fact
- Opinion
- Exclusive
- Copy
- Column
- Journalist
- Photograph
- Caption

Key Words Exercise

Work out the key words from the clues below, then find them in the word search.

H	I	T	E	E	H	S	D	A	O	R	B	V
E	D	N	E	T	W	E	R	I	L	E	D	W
A	A	E	F	S	O	V	O	E	A	V	N	O
D	E	S	A	S	A	I	T	Y	D	I	O	R
L	L	I	C	N	R	S	I	I	V	E	I	P
I	A	U	T	M	T	U	D	T	E	W	T	H
N	E	W	S	U	I	L	E	S	R	S	N	O
E	D	T	U	L	C	C	O	I	T	D	O	T
R	I	H	A	O	L	X	N	L	I	I	I	O
H	T	O	P	C	E	E	O	A	S	O	N	G
V	O	Y	H	E	A	L	I	N	E	L	I	R
I	R	E	P	O	R	T	T	R	M	B	P	A
W	I	D	J	O	U	R	P	U	E	A	O	P
B	A	N	N	E	R	I	A	O	N	T	E	H
T	L	O	N	Y	E	E	C	J	T	A	D	S

1. The main heading to a story or article.

2. Smaller format newspaper.

3. Large format newspaper.

4. Sometimes reports have these to illustrate them.

5. A reporter would submit one of these.

6. Things that are true.

7. Newspapers mainly report this.

8. A piece of writing on a particular topic is one of these.

9. Newspapers can include _____ on films and TV programmes.

10. A word that describes the newspaper's view on a key story or article.

11. The main purpose of these is to persuade people (maybe to buy something).

12. Another name for the material written by journalists.

13. The writing that explains a photograph.

14. Someone who writes for a newspaper.

15. A story that's only covered by one newspaper is called an _____ .

16. The main story of the newspaper.

17. Another name for the main, front page headline.

18. This person decides what to put in a newspaper.

19. Newspaper text is normally laid out in this format.

20. It's not a fact, but it may be true or false.

Testing Understanding

1 **Identify whether the following statements are true or false.**

a) Newspaper text is written in columns.

b) The writing that goes with a photograph is called a heading.

c) Some newspapers only cover local news.

d) The front page headline is called a poster.

e) Many newspapers contain sports news.

f) Journalists write material for newspapers.

g) The person who decides what news articles go into a newspaper is the editor.

h) Newspapers never contain advertisements.

i) Facts are things that are not true.

j) A news item published by only one paper is called an exclusive.

2 **Read the following newspaper report and identify the effects created by the sections of text, A–H.**

A **News Express**

Only 30p

B **JET SKIER TAKES OFF**

Rapid Response Rescue Plucks Jet Skier From Death

C A Sea Rescue helicopter plucked a jet skier from the sea in a dramatic rescue off the East Coast of Yorkshire yesterday afternoon. Two lifeboats were also involved in the rescue.

D Rob 'Rocket' Roberts was one of a group of jet skiers involved in a sponsored jet ski race down the East Coast. The race started at Scar Rock Harbour at 10.00 a.m. on Sunday morning. The sea was quite calm with a slight swell. An hour into the race, though, things changed drastically when a violent wind rose and sea conditions became horrendous. Most of the jet skiers managed to reach the shore, but Mr Roberts was hit by a huge, mountainous wave. His jet ski was smashed and he was thrown into the sea.

E 'I didn't know what hit me,' said Rob, 27, from Hartlepool. 'The wave was massive and came out of nowhere. It lifted me and the jet ski high in the air and then smashed us down, throwing me into the water and completely submerging the jet ski. Thank goodness for the rescue services.'

F Al Curtis, coxswain of the Scar Rock lifeboat, said that winds were gusting up to 28 knots with waves of 5 to 6 metres and that 'once in the water Mr Roberts was caught in a strong tidal current and would have been swept away if we hadn't reached him quickly'.

G Jet skiing is a popular and rapidly growing sport and the numbers taking part in the East Coast Race have grown in recent years. The race has been held annually since 2003 and this is the first time there have been any problems.

H Happily, all ended well and Mr Roberts is recovering well in hospital.

Write a newspaper report of your own.

Step 1: Choose a topic or subject for your report. For example, it could be based on...
- something that's happened to you
- an event that you've been involved in or heard about
- a report of a sports match, a school trip, etc.

Whatever subject you choose, make sure that you have enough information to write a report about it.

Step 2: Write down all the pieces of information that you're going to include in your report. If you have any direct comments from the people involved, include these here.

Step 3: Plan how you're going to structure your report:
- What you'll include in your introduction.
- The order that you're going to include the pieces of information.
- How you'll conclude your report.

Step 4: Write your report on a computer, creating a suitable and eye-catching headline. Lay your copy out in columns. Add pictures with captions to illustrate your report if you think these will make it more effective.

Extension Activity

1 Interviews are an important way for journalists or reporters to gather information for the reports and articles they write.

Step 1: Look at some interviews in newspapers and magazines or on the internet. You will find them on many different subjects, for example...
- celebrities
- sportsmen and women
- people who've done something unusual.

Step 2: Choose a friend or a member of your family and interview them about a particular topic or experience. For example, you could interview...
- an older relative about life in the past
- a friend who's taken part in a school production
- a friend or relative with an unusual hobby.

Step 3: Make a list of questions to ask. Be prepared to ask other questions when you're interviewing them if they say things you want to explore further.

Step 4: Record your interview with them.

2 Use this interview as the basis of a report or article.

Shakespeare

What is Covered in This Topic?

This topic looks at…
- the various types of plays Shakespeare wrote
- Shakespeare's characters
- how Shakespeare used soliloquies and asides
- Shakespeare's language.

Types of Shakespeare Plays

Shakespeare wrote his 38 plays between 1590 and 1613. He wrote many different kinds of plays about different situations and characters. His plays can be divided into these main types:

Tragedies Comedies
Histories Romances

Tragedies

In Shakespeare's **tragedies** the main character always dies at the end. Often, several other characters die or are killed too. Some of his best known tragedies are:
- *Romeo and Juliet*
- *Macbeth*
- *Othello*.

Comedies

A comedy is something that makes us laugh. Shakespeare's **comedies** contain very funny events and characters, but some contain very serious situations too. To Shakespeare's audience, a comedy ended happily, for example…
- *Twelfth Night*
- *A Midsummer Night's Dream*
- *The Merchant of Venice*.

Histories

The **histories** are plays about events and characters from history, usually kings or important leaders. Some well-known history plays are:
- *Richard III*
- *Henry V*
- *Julius Caesar*.

Romances

Romances are sometimes called Shakespeare's '**Last Plays**' because they were the last ones he wrote. These make use of fantasy or magic in their plots. Some well-known romance plays:
- *The Tempest*
- *The Winter's Tale*.

Twelfth Night

Twelfth Night is one of Shakespeare's comedies. The play is about identical twins Viola and her brother Sebastian. They are shipwrecked and become separated on the coast of Illyria.

The **plot** or storyline of the play is about the adventures that happen to the pair before they're reunited and involves disguise, mistaken identity and love.

The Structure of the Comedy

'**Structure**' is the word used to describe how the events of the play's storyline are arranged in a certain order. Shakespeare's comedies had a typical structure, which the play *Twelfth Night* follows:

1. Characters meet and fall in love.
2. Various things go wrong, such as mistaken identity.
3. The problems are all sorted out.
4. The play ends happily with the lovers together.

Learning About Characters

Characters are a key part of plays and we learn about them in various ways. In a play you can learn about characters by looking at...
- how a character behaves
- what the character says
- what other characters say about them.

💡 *Sir Toby Belch is one of the comic characters in* Twelfth Night. *What can you find out about him from these extracts from the play?*

1. *Maria: By my troth, Sir Toby, you must come in earlier o' nights.*
2. *Maria: That quaffing and drinking will undo you.*
3. *Sir Toby: With drinking health to my niece. I'll drink to her as long as there is a passage in my throat and drink in Illyria.*

Shakespeare

Soliloquies

One of the techniques Shakespeare uses to give us more information about a character is the **soliloquy**. This is a speech made by a character when they're alone on stage or when they seem to be talking directly to the audience.

A soliloquy can...
- let the audience know the character's thoughts and feelings
- let the audience know what the characters intend to do
- give information that other characters don't know.

Romeo and Juliet

In the tragedy *Romeo and Juliet*, Romeo falls in love at first sight with Juliet. This is an extract from Romeo's soliloquy as he walks alone in the orchard, beneath her window:

> But soft, what light through yonder window breaks?
>   It is the east, and Juliet is the sun.
> Arise fair sun and kill the envious moon,
>   Who is already sick and pale with grief
> That thou her maid art far more fair than she.
>   Be not her maid since she is envious.
> Her vestal livery is sick and green,
>   And none but fools wear it; cast it off.

Romeo compares Juliet to the sun – she is so much brighter than the moon, which is cold and pale in comparison.

In mythology, Diana was goddess of the moon and was served by maids dressed in 'vestal livery'.

💡 *Write your own modern version of what Romeo is saying in this soliloquy.*

Imagery

Shakespeare uses **imagery** to make Romeo's words more effective and dramatic. Imagery is a particular way of using language to make it more descriptive and powerful.

Metaphors and Similes

Shakespeare uses a particular type of imagery called a **metaphor** when he says that 'Juliet is the sun'.

A metaphor compares one thing to another. Unlike a **simile**, which would say Juliet is 'like' the sun, a metaphor actually says Juliet 'is' the sun. (These terms are covered in more detail in the next topic.)

Shakespeare also uses **personification**, which is when something that's not human is given human feelings or characteristics. For example, Shakespeare says that the moon is 'envious'.

💡 *What other examples of imagery can you see in this next part of Romeo's speech? You might find an example of...*
- *a simile*
- *a metaphor.*

The brightness of her cheek would shame those stars,
As daylight doth a lamp; her eyes in heaven
Would through the airy region stream so bright
That birds would sing, and think it were not night.

Quick Test

1. True or false – 'Arise fair sun and kill the envious moon' is a simile.
2. True or false – *The Tempest* is a history play.
3. True or false – Viola is a character in *Twelfth Night*.
4. True or false – *Romeo and Juliet* is a tragedy.
5. True or false – a soliloquy is meant to be heard only by the audience.

KEY WORDS
Make sure you understand these words before moving on!
- Tragedy
- Comedy
- History
- Romance
- Last plays
- Plot
- Structure
- Soliloquy
- Imagery
- Metaphor
- Simile
- Personification

Shakespeare

Key Words Exercise

Match each key word with its meaning.

Key word	Meaning
Simile	A kind of metaphor where something that's not human is described as if it has human feelings or qualities.
Plot	A comparison, using the words 'like' or 'as'.
Histories	Another term for Romances.
Metaphors	The way the action of a play is put together.
Romances	Plays with a happy ending.
Imagery	A comparison, saying that one thing actually is the other.
Soliloquy	The storyline of a play.
Comedies	Plays based on historical figures.
Structure	Plays that have a fantasy or magical element and were the last plays Shakespeare wrote.
Personification	What a character speaks while alone on stage.
Tragedies	The use of words to create a picture or 'image'.
Last plays	Plays that end with the death of the main character(s).

Anagrams

Use the following clues to unscramble each word.

1 The way a play is put together.   TRUCRUTES

2 A comparison using 'like' or 'as'.   ESMILI

3 A play about a Roman Emperor.   LUISJU RECSAA

4 'The sun smiled down on us' is an example of this.   FEARININOTIPOCS

5 These plays often include magic.   SAROMENC

Testing Understanding

1 **Are the following statements true or false?**

a) Shakespeare wrote 38 plays in all.

b) *Othello* is an example of a comedy.

c) Shakespeare's tragedies usually end with the death of the main character.

d) *The Merchant of Venice* is a comedy.

e) *Richard III* is a history play.

f) *The Tempest* is a tragedy.

g) Romeo is the hero of *Twelfth Night*.

h) Sir Toby Belch is a character in *A Midsummer Night's Dream*.

i) Viola in *Twelfth Night* has a twin brother.

j) In a soliloquy, a character speaks to the other characters in the play.

2 **Which of the following extracts are similes and which are metaphors?**

a) '…she hangs upon the cheek of night
Like a rich jewel in an Ethiop's ear.'   (*Romeo and Juliet*)

b) '…thou echoest me,
As if there were some monster in thy thought
Too hideous to be shown.'   (*Othello*)

c) 'If I catch him once upon the hip,
I will feed fat the ancient grudge I bear him.'   (*The Merchant of Venice*)

d) 'Death is my son-in-law, death is my heir,
My daughter he hath wedded.'   (*Romeo and Juliet*)

e) '…Although I joy in thee,
I have no joy of this contract tonight.
It is too rash, too unadvised, too sudden;
Too like the summer lightning, which doth cease to be
Ere one can say, "It lightens".'   (*Romeo and Juliet*)

she hangs upon the cheek of night Like a rich jewel in an Ethiop's ear.

Shakespeare

Skills Practice

Choose a Shakespeare play. You could pick a play you know and have studied before, or choose another one if you want to.

Step 1: Say what kind of play it is and write a brief summary of the plot. Find two soliloquies from the play and explain...

    a) where each soliloquy comes in the play

    b) who the speakers are

    c) what information, ideas, feelings, etc. they reveal to the audience

    d) what each soliloquy tells you about the character.

Step 2: Now find three examples of similes and three examples of metaphors from your play. Explain each example, writing about...

    a) what things are being compared

    b) the language Shakespeare uses

    c) the effects created by the simile or metaphor

    d) what you think about each one.

Extension Activity

Write a short information sheet for other students in your group, explaining what similes and metaphors are and the differences between them.

Illustrate your information sheet with examples from Shakespeare plays.

Present the information sheet to your class, explaining why you chose the examples that you used.

What is Covered in this Topic?

This topic looks at...
- the parts that make up a poem
- how imagery can help make a poem effective
- sound effects in poetry
- rhyme and rhythm.

Parts of a Poem

Poems are made up of language. Language can be used in many ways to express different ideas. In a poem, the language and ideas combine to make the poem effective.

Here are some of the parts that make up a poem:

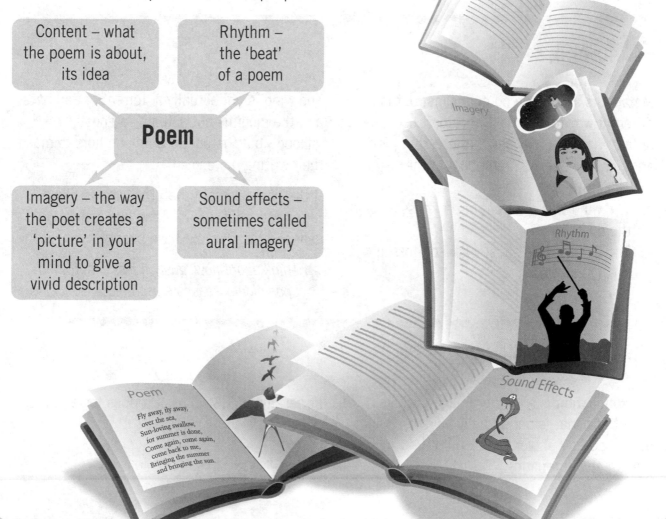

Content – what the poem is about, its idea

Rhythm – the 'beat' of a poem

Poem

Imagery – the way the poet creates a 'picture' in your mind to give a vivid description

Sound effects – sometimes called aural imagery

Imagery

Rhythm

Sound Effects

Poem

Fly away, fly away,
over the sea,
Sun-loving swallow,
for summer is done,
Come again, come again,
come back to me,
Bringing the summer
and bringing the sun.

Reading Poetry

Imagery

When poets use language to create a 'picture' of what they're describing, it is called **imagery**. It is also sometimes called figurative language.

Similes

Similes are when one thing is compared to another to make a description more vivid.

This helps the reader to imagine and picture it in their mind. Similes are used all the time in everyday speech.

For example...
- daft as a brush
- white as a sheet
- dropped like a stone
- slept like a log.

Poetic similes are a more interesting and original simile. Similes always use 'like' or 'as' to make the comparison.

Metaphors

Metaphors also make comparisons, but in a different way to similes. They don't use 'like' or 'as' – instead they say that one thing *is* another. Look at the metaphors in the following lines:
- The wind was a torrent of darkness among the dusty trees.
- The moon was a ghostly galleon tossed upon cloudy seas.

The wind is not actually a 'torrent of darkness' and the moon is not actually 'a ghostly galleon', but the poet uses metaphors to make their writing more vivid.

If the poet had said that 'the wind is like a torrent', or that 'the moon is like a ghostly galleon', these would have become similes.

Think about how 'gusty trees' and 'tossed upon cloudy seas' are used metaphorically.

Personification

Personification is a kind of imagery where something that is not actually alive is described as if it were a person or had human characteristics.

For example, T.S. Eliot describes fog as though it were a person:

The yellow fog that rubs its back upon the window panes

Sound Effects

Rather than creating a picture in the mind with words, the use of sound effects can create imagery and make a description more vivid.

This is called **aural** imagery. The **techniques** a writer can use to create sound effects are...
- alliteration
- assonance
- onomatopoeia.

Alliteration

Alliteration is created by the repetition of words with the same **consonant**.

A consonant is any letter other than the **vowels** 'a', 'e', 'i', 'o', and 'u'. The following example uses alliteration by repeating the letter 'w':

> He wandered alone in the wet, wild, wilderness.

What effect do you think this repetition has?

Assonance

Assonance is similar to alliteration but it uses the repetition of vowel sounds. For example:

> The curfew tolls the knell of parting day,
> The lowing herd winds slowly o'er the lea

The repeated long 'o' sound gives a feeling of the weariness at the end of the day.

Onomatopoeia

Onomatopoeia is when a word sounds like the sound it is describing, for example...
- bang
- crash
- hiss
- plop.

Reading Poetry

Rhyme

Rhyme can have an important effect on the sound of a poem. Words at the ends of lines usually rhyme, although sometimes lines can rhyme within a line – this is called internal rhyme.

The pattern of rhyme within a poem is called the **rhyme scheme**. You can work out this pattern by looking at which lines rhyme together.

💡 *Which lines rhyme in the following Christina Rossetti poem, The Swallow?*

Fly away, fly away, over the sea,	A
Sun-loving swallow, for summer is done,	B
Come again, come again, come back to me,	A
Bringing the summer and bringing the sun.	B

You'll have noticed that the first and third lines, and the second and fourth lines, rhyme, so this is an ABAB rhyme scheme.

💡 *Think about the effect this rhyme scheme has on the poem.*

Rhythm

Rhythm is the beat or tempo of a poem.

The rhythm can create a sense of movement in a poem to suit the setting, tone or mood of the poem. It might be slow or plodding, or it might give a strong impression of movement, as in this example:

I sprang to the stirrup, and Joris, and he;
I galloped, Dirk galloped, we galloped all three;
'Good speed!' cried the watch, as the gate bolts undrew,
'Speed!' echoed the wall to us galloping through.

It is not only important that you can spot these features, but being able to say something about the effects they create.

💡 *Read a poem aloud, tapping out the beat of the words as you read them.*

Quick Test

1. Name three different kinds of imagery.
2. What is the name of the kind of imagery that uses sound effects?
3. What is 'slipping and sliding down the slope' an example of?
4. What sounds is assonance the repetition of?
5. What is 'Bang!' an example of?

Key Words Exercise

Work out the key words from the clues below, then copy and complete the crossword.

Across

2. The 'beat' of a poem. (6)
7. 'The wind cut through me' is an example of this. (8)
9. 'E' is an example of one of these. (5)
11. Similes and metaphors are examples of this. (7)
12. Describing something that's not alive as if it's a person. (15)
13. Poets use a variety of these to create effects. (10)
14. 'Tremendous tumbling torrent' is an example of this. (12)

Down

1. The rhyme pattern of a poem. (6)
3. 'Like' or 'as' is usually used in these. (6)
4. Not a vowel. (9)
5. 'Bang!', 'Crash!' and 'Thud!' are examples of this. (12)
6. Some poems do this, some poems don't. (5)
8. The repetition of vowel sounds. (9)
10. This kind of imagery uses sounds. (5)

Reading Poetry

Testing Understanding

1 **Carefully read the following poem by Andrew Young.**

Identify an example of each of the following techniques in the poem:
  a) A metaphor
  b) A simile
  c) Onomatopoeia
  d) Personification
  e) A rhyme scheme.

Hard Frost

Frost called to water 'Halt!'
And crusted the moist snow with sparkling salt;
Brooks, their own bridges, stop,
And icicles in long stalactites drop,
And tench in water-holes
Lurk under gluey glass like fish in bowls.

In the hard-rutted lane
At every footstep breaks a brittle pane,
And tinkling trees ice-bound
Changed into weeping willows, sweep the ground;
Dead boughs take root in ponds
And ferns on windows shoot their ghostly fronds.

But vainly the fierce frost
Inters poor fish, ranks trees in an armed host,
Hangs daggers from house-eaves
And on the windows ferny ambush weaves;
In the long war grown warmer
The sun will strike him dead and strip his armour.

Carefully read the following Ted Hughes poem, *Football at Slack.*

Football at Slack

Between plunging valleys, on a bareback of hill
Men in bunting colours
Bounced, and their blown ball bounced.

The blown ball jumped, and the merry-coloured men
Spouted like water to head it.
The ball blew away downward -

The rubbery men bounced after it.
The ball blew jumped up and out and hung on the wind
Over a gulf of treetops.
Then they all shouted together, and the ball blew back.

Winds from fiery holes in heaven
Piled the hills darkening around them
To awe them. The glare light
Mixed its mad oils and threw glooms.
Then the rain lowered a steel press.

Hair plastered, they all just trod water
To puddle glitter. And their shouts bobbed up
Coming fine and thin, washed and happy

While the humped world sank foundering
And the valleys blued unthinkable
Under depth of Atlantic depression -

But the wingers leapt, they bicycled in air
And the goalie flew horizontal

And once again a golden holocaust
Lifted the cloud's edge, to watch them.

Now write about your thoughts and ideas on the poem. Focus on the following ideas:
- What the poem's about.
- The use of metaphors.
- The use of similes.
- The use of aural imagery.
- The use of particular word and phrases.

Remember that when writing about a poem it's important to not only identify words, phrases, metaphors, similes, etc., but also to write about the effects they create in your mind.

Extension Activity

Working with a partner, each choose a poem of your own and study it carefully. Then swap poems and read your partner's poem.

Write down at least four questions about the poem to ask your partner. Try to ask questions about the language and techniques used rather than just what the poem's about.

Ask your partner your questions and discuss the poem between you. Then answer your partner's questions on your poem and discuss your ideas together.

Punctuation

This topic looks at...
- direct speech
- reported speech
- play scripts.

Direct Speech

Direct speech is when the actual spoken words are used in a piece of writing. This kind of writing speech has its own special kind of **punctuation**.

Look carefully at the way the following piece of speech is punctuated.

The Hobbit by J.R.R. Tolkien

'Something strange is happening,' said Thorin. 'The time has gone for the autumn wanderings; and these are birds that dwell always in the land; there are starlings and flocks of finches; and far off there are many carrion birds as if a battle were afoot!'

Suddenly Bilbo pointed: 'There is that old thrush again!' he cried. 'He seems to have escaped, when Smaug smashed the mountain-side, but I don't suppose the snails have!'

Sure enough the old thrush was there, and as Bilbo pointed, he flew towards them and perched on a stone near by. Then he fluttered his wings and sang; then he cocked his head on one side, as if to listen; and again he sang, and again he listened.

'I believe he is trying to tell us something,' said Balin; 'but I cannot follow the speech of such birds, it is very quick and difficult. Can you make it out, Baggins?'

'Not very well,' said Bilbo (as a matter of fact, he could making nothing of it at all); 'but the old fellow seems very excited.'

'I only wish he was a raven!' said Balin.

'I thought you did not like them! You seemed very shy of them, when we came this way before.'

1. Speech marks only go around the words that are actually being spoken.

2. A comma is needed to separate the spoken part from the part telling you who is speaking, unless a question mark or exclamation is used.

3. If an exclamation mark or a question mark is used, then a comma's not needed to separate the spoken words from the rest.

4. A capital letter isn't needed here because this is a continuation of the spoken sentence.

5. Speech begins with a capital letter at the beginning of the spoken sentence.

6. A new paragraph's needed every time a different speaker begins speaking.

Speech Layout

There are three different kinds of speech layout (the spoken words are highlighted in italics):

- The part telling you who is speaking comes at the end, e.g. *'Are you coming to my party, Kim?'* asked Jane.
- The part telling you who is speaking comes at the beginning, e.g. Kim said, *'Yes, I'm really looking forward to it.'*
- The part telling you who's speaking comes in the middle of the speech sentence, e.g. *'That's great,'* said Jane, *'because you'll know lots of the others that are coming.'*

If in doubt where to place the **speech marks**, ask yourself what words are being spoken. These are the words that need speech marks (also called **quotation marks**) around them.

Indirect Speech

Indirect speech (sometimes called **reported speech**) is a different way of writing down things that have been said. The following conversation is written in direct speech:

'What are you doing?' the farmer asked Matt and his friends.

'We know we shouldn't be here,' answered Matt, 'but we're not doing any harm.'

'Where are the rest of your friends now, and what are they doing?' The farmer looked at him suspiciously.

'I don't know, but I expect they're hiding in the woods.'

'What are you doing in this barn?'

'We're looking for shelter from the rain.'

'But you shouldn't be on my land at all,' said the farmer, beginning to get angry. 'The police are on their way.'

'I'm sorry,' Matt said.

Here is the same conversation written in indirect speech:

The farmer asked Matt what he was doing. Matt answered that he knew they shouldn't have been there but they weren't doing any harm. The farmer asked him where the rest of his friends were and Matt replied that he didn't know, but that they'd probably hidden in the woods.

The farmer then asked Matt what they were doing in the barn and Matt replied that they were looking for shelter from the rain.

The farmer began to get angry and told Matt that they shouldn't have been on his land at all and that the police were on their way. Matt apologised.

Think about the changes that have been made to change the direct speech version into the indirect speech version.

Punctuation

Changing Pronouns

When the conversation is converted from direct speech to indirect speech, several changes occur.

First and second person personal **pronouns** are changed to the third person.

Direct Speech	Indirect Speech
You (singular)	He / She
Your	His / Her
We	They
I	He / She
You (plural)	They
My	His / Her

Changing Tense and Adverbs

The **tense** is changed, mainly from the **present** (direct speech) to the **past** (indirect speech), for example...
- 'What are you doing?' (direct); What he was doing (indirect).
- 'Shouldn't be on my land' (direct); Should not have been on his land (indirect).

The **adverbs** that refer to time and space change. Phrases such as 'said the farmer', are changed to 'The farmer said that...,' for example...
- here (direct) – there (indirect)
- now (direct) – then (indirect)
- this (direct) – that (indirect).

Word order can change and some information can be summarised:
- Direct speech – 'I'm sorry,' said Matt.
- Indirect speech – Matt apologised; speech marks aren't used.

PRIVATE ROAD NO TRESPASSING

Play Scripts

Play scripts (sometimes called **drama** scripts) are another way of presenting speech.

Look at the following example of a short play script.

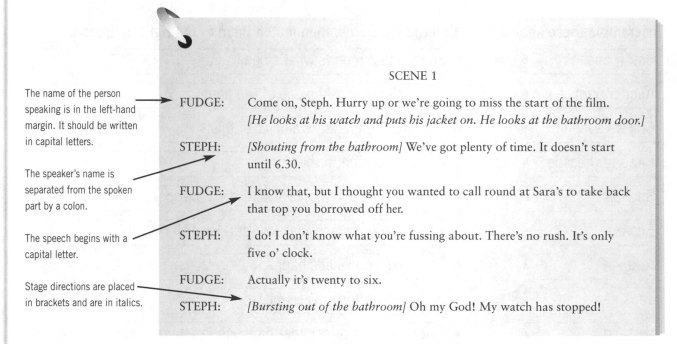

The name of the person speaking is in the left-hand margin. It should be written in capital letters.

The speaker's name is separated from the spoken part by a colon.

The speech begins with a capital letter.

Stage directions are placed in brackets and are in italics.

SCENE 1

FUDGE: Come on, Steph. Hurry up or we're going to miss the start of the film. *[He looks at his watch and puts his jacket on. He looks at the bathroom door.]*

STEPH: *[Shouting from the bathroom]* We've got plenty of time. It doesn't start until 6.30.

FUDGE: I know that, but I thought you wanted to call round at Sara's to take back that top you borrowed off her.

STEPH: I do! I don't know what you're fussing about. There's no rush. It's only five o' clock.

FUDGE: Actually it's twenty to six.

STEPH: *[Bursting out of the bathroom]* Oh my God! My watch has stopped!

The example shows that...
- speech marks aren't used in play scripts
- the name of the character speaking is on the left-hand side
- the speaker's name is separated from the spoken part by a colon
- the speech begins with a capital letter
- **stage directions** are used to describe actions, scenes and anything else happening on the stage; they're usually brief and aren't spoken, so they're put in brackets and in italics.

Quick Test

1. What are used in direct speech, but not in indirect speech and play scripts?
2. When writing direct speech, when should you begin a new line?
3. In what tense is indirect speech usually written?
4. In a play script, what separates the speaker's name from what they say?
5. What do stage directions do?

KEY WORDS
Make sure you understand these words before moving on!
- Direct speech
- Punctuation
- Speech mark
- Quotation mark
- Indirect speech
- Reported speech
- Pronoun
- Tense
- Present
- Past
- Adverb
- Play script
- Drama
- Stage direction

Punctuation

Unscramble these anagrams to find the key words, then match them to the right definition.

Credit cheeps	Speech that reports what's been said.
Auctionpunt	Words that stand in place of the noun.
Crinedt secpeh	Past and present are examples of this.
Deporter hecspe	A play is written in this.
Snoopurn	Speech that uses the exact words that are spoken.
Enset	These marks help to make written English readable.
Restpen	These tell you what's happening on stage.
Taps neets	Another term for 'play script'.
Verbsad	This describes things that happened yesterday, for example.
Layp prisct	Another term for 'speech marks'.
Amard crispt	The tense that describes things that are happening now.
Peshce krams	These only go round the words that are spoken.
Tuqootain skarm	Another term for 'indirect speech'.
Getsa creditsoin	Words that tell you more about the verb.

Testing Understanding

1 **a)** Write out the following passage, putting in the speech marks where necessary and laying the speech out correctly.

> A Merry Christmas, Uncle! God save you! cried a cheerful voice. It was the voice of Scrooge's nephew, who came upon him so quickly that this was the first intimation he had of his approach. Bah! said Scrooge, Humbug! He had so heated himself with rapid walking in the fog and frost, this nephew of Scrooge's, that he was all in a glow; his face was ruddy and handsome; his eyes sparkled, and his breath smoked again. Christmas a humbug, uncle! said Scrooge's nephew. You don't mean that, I am sure? I do, said Scrooge. Merry Christmas! What right have you to be merry? What reason have you to be merry? You're poor enough. Come, then, returned the nephew gaily. What right have you to be dismal? What reason have you to be morose? You're rich enough.
>
> *A Christmas Carol* by Charles Dickens

b) Now try writing out the passage again, converting it into indirect speech.

c) Convert your direct speech version of this extract into play script form.

Punctuation

Record a short conversation between yourself and a friend, or with a member of your family.

Step 1: Write out the conversation in direct speech. Think about...
- the layout – use a new paragraph for a new speaker
- where the speech marks should go
- the use of capital letters
- the use of punctuation marks such as commas, full stops, question marks and exclamation marks.

Step 2: Write another version of this using indirect speech. Remember to think about...
- your use of tense
- changing pronouns
- changing adverbs
- changing phrases such as 'said the girl'
- removing speech marks.

Step 3: Compare the differences between your two versions.

Extension Activity

Working with a partner or small group, write a short scene for a play.

The scene can be about anything you like. Focus on...
- the layout of the speech
- the use of stage directions
- using the correct tense.

When you've finished writing the scene, try performing it. Use your script to act it out, with each person taking a part and one person acting as director to take control of the action.

...u need to...
...apture a sense of the characters' voices
...ake use of your stage directions.

...ber that you'll need to practise this several
...d experiment with different ways of speaking
...nd acting out the action.

Spelling

What is Covered in this Topic?

This topic covers...
- forming plurals of **nouns**
- commonly confused words.

Forming Plurals

Your **spelling** should be **accurate** to make your writing as effective as possible.

Spelling mistakes often happen when making **singular** nouns into **plurals**. Plurals are formed in different ways.

Regular Plurals

Many nouns are made plural simply by adding an 's', for example...
- car(s)
- computer(s)
- floor(s)
- window(s)
- chair(s)
- desk(s)
- pencil(s)
- tree(s).

tree

trees

Sibilants

Nouns ending with 's' or 'sh' sounds are called **sibilants**. Add 'es' unless the word ends in 'e'. If the word ends in 'e', then only an 's' is needed. For example...
- torch(es)
- prize(s)
- fox(es)
- house(s)
- bus(es)
- hose(s).

fox

foxes

Spelling

Nouns Ending in Y

To find the ending for nouns that end in 'y', look at the letter before the 'y'.

If the letter is a **consonant** (any letter other than 'a', 'e', 'i', 'o', 'u'), change the 'y' to 'ies', for example...

- body – bodies
- party – parties
- lady – ladies
- century – centuries
- baby – babies
- puppy – puppies
- city – cities
- army – armies
- sky – skies
- apply – applies.

(Note that this rule doesn't apply to proper nouns.)

If the letter before the 'y' is a **vowel** ('a', 'e', 'i', 'o', 'u'), add 's', for example...

- alley(s)
- tray(s)
- key(s)
- play(s)
- ray(s)
- donkey(s)
- chimney(s)
- day(s).

donkeys

donkey

Nouns Ending in O

You need to learn which words end in 's' and which end in 'es' with this kind of plural.

If a singular noun ends in 'o', normally the word is turned into a plural by adding an 's', for example...

- (s)

There are some exceptions when 'es' is needed, for example...

- echo(es)
- tomato(es)
- hero(es)
- torpedo(es)
- potato(es)
- tornado(es).

Nouns Ending in F and Fe

If a singular noun ends in 'f', change the 'f' to 'v' and add 'es', for example...
- loaf – loaves
- thief – thieves
- half – halves
- yourself – yourselves.

If a singular noun ends in 'fe', the plural ends in 'ves', for example...
- knife – knives
- life – lives
- wife – wives.

Not all words follow this pattern, for example...
- roof – roofs
- handkerchief – handkerchiefs
- chief – chiefs
- belief – beliefs.

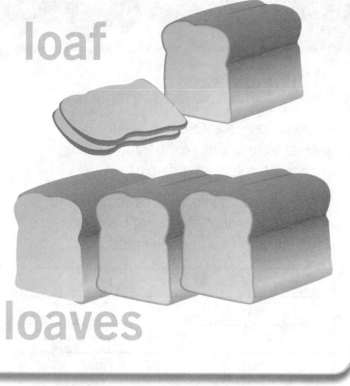

loaf

loaves

Unusual Plural Nouns

Not all plural nouns end in 's' or 'es'. With some nouns the word can be used to mean either the singular or plural, for example...
- I saw a deer in the wood (singular)
- I saw three deer in the wood (plural).

Some other examples of this kind of singular or plural noun are...
- sheep
- trout
- salmon.

Some nouns change their spelling when they're changed to plural, for example...
- foot – feet
- tooth – teeth
- mouse – mice.

Other nouns are only ever used in the plural, for example...
- scissors
- trousers
- clothes.

Collective nouns are unusual because they're singular nouns that mean a group of things, for example, a herd (singular – one herd) of cows (plural – more than one cow).

mice

mouse

Spelling

Homophones

A **homophone** is a word that **sounds** like another word but has a different **meaning**. They're often spelled differently.

Some common words are often muddled up because they sound the same, but they have different meanings and spellings:

Pair	Pear
Tow	Toe
Waist	Waste
Here	Hear
There	Their
Manor	Manner
Flower	Flour
Fowl	Foul
Bear	Bare
Whether	Weather
Seems	Seams
Hair	Hare

💡 Look up the meaning of each of the words in a **dictionary**.

flour

flower

ick Test

mpete the following sentence: Spelling
akes are often made when making
lar words into _____ .
re nouns with 's' or 'sh' sounds called?
me is given to words that sound the
have a different meaning?
plural of deer?
you do if in doubt about the
aning of a word?

KEY WORDS
Make sure you understand these words
before moving on!
- Noun
- Spelling
- Accurate
- Singular
- Plural
- Sibilant
- Consonant
- Vowel
- Collective noun
- Homophone
- Sounds
- Meaning
- Dictionary

Key Words Exercise

Choose the correct options in the following sentences.

1. When writing, your spelling should be as **interesting** / **accurate** / **detailed** as possible.

2. If you're writing about one person or object, you're writing in the **plural** / **first person** / **singular**.

3. The letters 'm', 'p', and 't' are all **vowels** / **adjectives** / **consonants**.

4. A noun that names a group of people or object is called an **abstract** / **proper** / **collective** noun.

5. It's important that your **spelling** / **sentence** / **dictionary** is correct so that your writing is clear.

6. The words 'weather' and 'whether' are examples of **proper nouns** / **homophones** / **sibilance**.

7. The letters 'a', 'e', 'i', 'o', and 'u' are **vowels** / **consonants** / **homophones**.

8. The word 'sibilance' describes a certain kind of **image** / **meaning** / **sound**.

9. Words that name things are called **verbs** / **nouns** / **adjectives**.

10. You use **spellings** / **singular** / **plurals** when writing about more than one person or thing.

11. Good spelling helps to make your **vowels** / **nouns** / **meaning** clear.

12. If you're unsure about a spelling, use a **book** / **sound** / **dictionary** to check it.

13. The phrase 'the slithering, slinky snake' uses **onomatopoeia** / **sibilance** / **noises** to create sound effects.

Spelling

1 Complete the plural ending in each of the following sentences.

a) Sophie always found the English class really interesting.

b) The removal men loaded all the box into the van.

c) The geography teacher asked Alex to give out the atlas.

d) All the table were ready in the restaurant.

e) Jim was very hot, so he opened all the window.

f) The house were empty and due to be demolished.

g) Tim was three inch shorter than his brother.

h) The ray from the sun were very strong.

2 Correct the spellings in the following sentences.

a) The boyes both had several hobbys, including football and skateboarding.

b) One of Alice's qualitys was that she was hardworking and always made the best of her opportunitys.

c) My mother made a delicious curry with mangos and tomatos.

d) The soldieres were all heros in their own ways.

e) There were lots of mosquitos, as the whether was to hot.

f) Alan's trouseres were a little tight on his waste after he ate a huge pile of potatos.

g) The ship was being toed and steered a careful course between the boys.

h) The sopranoes, singing beautifully, were dressed like angels with their halos gleaming in the lightes.

3 Write out the following passage, correcting all the spelling mistakes as you do.

Todd and his friendes followed the path into the valley. The heards of cattle roamed freely and there were lots of sheeps too. All manor of birdes flew in the sky and Todd and his frends felt the sun on there faces and the wind gently ruffle there hare. They had herd that bares roamed these hills but they didn't sea any and so thought they must be in there lairs. In the streams they sore trouts swimming and salmons jumping.

Skills Practice

Working in small groups, look through the exercise book or folder of work of each member of your group. Pick two or three pieces to look at.

Step 1:   Look at pieces of work that have been marked and corrected by your teacher. Make a list of all the spelling mistakes that have been spotted.

Step 2:   Try to put the mistakes into groups according to what the problem is, for example...
- plural endings
- homophones
- confused words
- a wrong spelling for some other reason.

Step 3:   Make a table or graph showing the most common spelling mistakes.

Step 4:   Produce a large poster showing...
- each spelling error (give the word in its context of a phrase or sentence)
- the correct spelling
- pictures or illustrations to add impact and effect to your poster.

Extension Activity

Choose a problem from this topic that can occur in spelling (e.g. making plurals of nouns, homophones).

Prepare a PowerPoint presentation, illustrating the kinds of mistakes that are often made and say why. Your presentation should...
- give examples of words that are often spelt wrong
- give the correct spellings of these words in a sentence
- include a short spelling test.

Give your presentation to your class or a small group.

Include the spelling test and see how well your audience does.

Reading for Meaning

What is Covered in This Topic?

This topic looks at...
- different kinds of non-fiction texts
- analysing the content of non-fiction texts
- analysing how non-fiction texts use language
- approaching your own analysis.

Non-fiction texts

The term **non-fiction** covers a wide range of different kinds of writing and usually contains **factual information**. Non-fiction texts can include the following:
- Non-fiction
- Newspapers
- Guidebooks
- Reports
- Information from websites
- Magazine articles
- Text books
- Travel writing
- Autobiographies
- Biographies.

How many other kinds of non-fiction texts can you think of?

Reading Texts

When reading a text you should think about...
- the **content**, ideas and issues
- the way that language is used (sometimes called **style**)
- the way the information is **presented** – sometimes **texts** use diagrams, pictures or **illustrations** to add effect to the writing
- your own thoughts and responses to it.

Examining Non-fiction

Below is a non-fiction text about global warming. Read it carefully and jot down your ideas about...

- the **ideas** expressed (the **topic** or content)
- the ways that language is used, with examples
- the way in which the information's presented
- your views on the content and the way it's presented.

How effective do you think this piece is? Does it get its message across effectively?

Climate Change for Kids

Global Warming

Lots of people have studied the climate all around the world. They agreed several years ago that climate change really was happening. As a result, all countries in the world came together in a big conference at Kyoto in Japan.

Here they began to try and agree what to do about climate change. Lots of promises were made but countries haven't been very good at carrying them out.

Since then, the evidence of change has become stronger and stronger. The special computer 'models' which scientists had used have become more and more accurate. The ice sheets in both the Arctic and the Antarctic are melting, in some cases very fast. Sea levels are rising.

Temperatures are rising, especially in the Arctic and Antarctic. Glaciers on other mountains of the world are melting very fast – especially in the Himalayas. Animals and plants which like warmer conditions are moving further north and south. Yes, it's happening all right.

The world is hotting up. And I'm sorry to say it's all people's fault.

Reading for Meaning

Examining Non-Fiction (cont.)

In the passage from the *Climate Change for Kids* website, you might have noticed some of the following ideas and techniques used.

Title	The title, *Climate Change for Kids*, is aimed at a younger **audience** and makes the topic of the piece immediately clear.
Quotation	The quotation about how the ice will affect the polar bear has a 'shock' effect – it makes you think about the seriousness of climate change using a very specific example.
Background information	Some background to climate change is given with mention of Kyoto. The emphasis is on the idea that little has been done and that temperatures continue to rise.
Examples	Examples of the effects of global warming are given, e.g. 'Glaciers... are melting very fast', 'Sea levels are rising'.
Informal style	The language and style is quite informal. The use of words like 'lots' and contractions such as 'haven't' makes it appeal more to its target audience, which in this case is young people.
Illustrations	The use of pictures and cartoons to illustrate the text add to its impact. The cartoons illustrate some key points in the text but in a way that emphasises the serious message.

Writing Your Own Analysis of a Text

The following steps show one approach you can use when writing your own **analysis** of a text:

1. Look at the title of the piece of writing. This gives an immediate indication of what the writing's about. Read the text to get a general idea of the topic.

2. Read through the text to get ideas of what it's about, what points it makes, opinions expressed, etc. Think about the audience it's aimed at and the **purpose**.

3. Re-read the text carefully and make a note of the key points the writer makes.

4. Think about how language is used to suit the audience and purpose. Give specific details of the use of language and **comment** on the **effects** created.

5. Think about the effects of any headings, pictures, photographs, captions, illustrations, etc.

Make sure you use the PEE approach when writing an analysis:

- **Point** – make a point.
- **Evidence** – give an example.
- **Explanation** – comment on its effects, explain the significance, etc.

Quick Test

1. What kind of information does non-fiction usually contain?
2. Complete the following sentence:
   The way that language is used is called _____ .
3. What is it called when you look carefully at how language is used?
4. What does the term PEE approach stand for?

Reading for Meaning

Key Words Exercise

Work out the key words from the clues below, then find them in the word search.

E	C	N	E	D	I	V	E	Z	S	F	L	A	U	N
Q	B	I	G	T	E	X	T	S	N	R	V	G	I	O
V	A	D	N	A	G	A	N	P	O	U	R	E	N	I
K	J	E	W	M	P	E	I	V	I	B	Q	S	N	T
P	B	A	E	P	J	F	A	C	T	U	A	L	O	A
C	D	S	S	T	Y	L	E	L	A	A	V	E	I	N
C	O	I	Z	U	L	F	Z	D	R	I	A	Z	T	A
L	T	N	V	S	F	B	R	E	T	H	N	L	C	L
C	B	N	T	E	K	P	Q	T	S	L	A	M	I	P
I	V	R	C	E	R	J	E	N	U	Q	L	T	F	X
P	H	T	I	A	N	W	S	E	L	I	Y	N	N	E
O	P	S	N	R	G	T	N	S	L	F	S	I	O	H
T	D	X	L	Y	Z	O	I	E	I	A	I	O	N	Y
A	U	D	I	E	N	C	E	R	E	R	S	P	R	T
A	S	R	M	D	O	E	A	P	T	O	P	C	S	N

1 The opposite kind of writing to that in a novel or short story.

2 When analysing writing, what approach should you use? (3 words)

3 When looking at a piece of writing you need to identify its _____ and its _____ .

4 When you write about how language is used and the effects that it creates, you're writing an _____ .

5 In writing a piece a writer often uses a particular _____ of writing.

6 Things like headings and pictures can add to the way a piece of writing is _____ .

7 The theme or subject of a piece of writing.

8 Non-fiction writing is often _____ information.

9 What does non-fiction writing contain?

10 What are pieces of writing often called?

11 Writers often express their _____ in their writing.

12 What is another word for pictures or diagrams?

13 The material in a piece of writing is called its _____ .

Read the following extract carefully. It's taken from the Bullying UK website giving advice to young people about bullying.

○ ○ ○
◄ ► ⌂ C + http//:www.bullying.co.uk

introductiontobullying

We all know that bullying goes on in every school but it's the way it's dealt with which makes the difference between life being tolerable or a misery. Bullies are very cunning and are expert at getting away with it.

Bullying includes:
- People calling you names
- Making things up to get you into trouble
- Hitting, pinching, biting, pushing and shoving
- Taking things away from you
- Spreading rumours
- Threats and intimidation
- Damaging your belongings
- Stealing your money
- Taking your friends away from you
- Posting insulting messages on the internet or by IM (cyberbullying)

How to solve the problem

If you are being bullied, tell a friend, tell a teacher and tell your parents. It won't stop unless you do. It can be hard to do this so if you don't feel you can do it in person it might be easier to write a note to your parents explaining how you feel, or perhaps confide in someone outside the immediate family, like a grandparent, aunt, uncle or cousin and ask them to help you tell your parents what's going on.

Your form tutor needs to know what is going on so try to find a time to tell him / her when it won't be noticeable. You could stay behind on the pretext of needing help with some work. If you don't feel you can do that, then go to the medical room and speak to the school nurse.

The best idea is if a teacher can catch the bullies red-handed. That way, you won't get into bother from anyone for telling tales. It will be clear to everyone what has been going on. Don't be tempted to hit back because you could get hurt or get into trouble. Hitting someone is an assault.

Try to stay in safe areas of the school at break and lunchtime where there are plenty of other people. Bullies don't like witnesses. If you are hurt at school, tell a teacher immediately and ask for it to be written down. Make sure you tell your parents.

a) Identify the audience and purpose for this piece of writing.
b) What key thing does the writer say someone being bullied should do?
c) Name three kinds of bullying that might take place.
d) How does the writer try to encourage anyone being bullied to tell someone about it?
e) What kind of language does the writer use?
f) Does the way the information is presented help you to follow it?

Reading for Meaning

Write your own analysis of a text.

Choose a piece of non-fiction writing to use as the basis of a written analysis. Don't choose too long a piece (250 to 300 words will be fine). You could pick a piece from a text book, magazine or the internet or anywhere else you choose.

Write about…
- the audience and purpose of the writing
- the key point or points that the writer is making
- how the writer presents the information
- the way language is used and give examples of this.

Remember to use this method:
- Point
- Evidence
- Explanation.

Extension Activity

Talk to a friend about a film or TV programme that you've recently seen. See if your views and ideas are the same or if they differ in any way.

Write down the main points your friend makes and your own ideas too.

Use the ideas from this as the basis of a review on the film or TV programme.

Write your review and then let your friend read it; discuss his or her responses to it.

Index

A
Adjectives 6, 13, 19
Adverbs 6, 19, 68
Alliteration 61
Articles 20
Assonance 61
Atmosphere 14
Audience 24–27
Aural imagery 61

C
Characters 4, 11–12, 53
Conjunctions 20
Consonant 74
Counter argument 32

D
Dialogue 6
Direct speech 66

E
Emphasis 32

F
Fact 33
First person narrative 6, 7

H
Homophone 76

I
Imagery 55, 60
Indirect speech 67
Information 38
Interjections 20

L
Language 4, 14

M
Metaphor 13, 55, 60

N
Narrative viewpoint 6
Newspapers 45–48
Non-fiction 80–83
Nouns 19, 73, 74

O
Onomatopoeia 61
Opinion 33

P
PEE approach 83
Personification 55, 60
Planning 4
Play scripts 69
Plot 4, 53
Plural nouns 73–75
Poetry 59–62
Presenting techniques
    39–41
Pronouns 19, 68
Propositions 20
Punctuation 66
Purpose 24–27, 38

R
Rhetorical question 32
Rhyme 62
Rhythm 62

S
Setting 4, 13
Shakespeare's plays
    52–55
Sibilants 73
Simile 13, 55, 60
Soliloquy 54

Stereotypes 11
Structure 4, 5, 34, 53
Style 4

T
Tense 68
Themes 4
Third person narrative 6, 7

V
Verbs 19
Viewpoint 31
Vowel 74

W
Word classes 18

ACKNOWLEDGEMENTS

The authors and publisher are grateful to the copyright holders for permission to use quoted materials and images.

P.4   ©iStockphoto.com / Charity Myers
      ©iStockphoto.com / Rodrigo Eustachio
P.5   ©iStockphoto.com
      Extract from *Someone Like You* by Roald Dahl, published by Penguin Books Ltd. Reproduced by permission of Higham Associates
      Extract from *STONE COLD* by Robert Swindells (Hamish Hamilton, 1993) Copyright © Robert Swindells, 1993.
      Extract from *The Red Room* by H G Wells. A P Watt Ltd on behalf of The Literary Executors of the Estate of H G Wells.
P.6   © iStockphoto.com / Rodrigo Eustachio
P.7   ©iStockphoto.com / Joshua Blake
P.9   ©iStockphoto.com
P.11 ©iStockphoto.com / Charity Myers
P.12 Extract from *Nightmare Stairs* by Robert Swindells, published by Corgi. Reprinted by permission of The Random House Group Ltd
      Extract from *The Secret Passage* by Nina Bawden. Reprinted by permission of Curtis Brown Group Ltd
P.13 ©iStockphoto.com / Charity Myers
      Lord of the Flies (1954) by William Golding. Extract reprinted by permission of the publisher, Faber and Faber Ltd., London
P.15 ©iStockphoto.com
P.16 Extract from *The Watch House* by Robert Westall. Reprinted by permission of Macmillan Publishers Ltd.
P.24 ©iStockphoto.com / Joshua Blake
      © iStockphoto.com
      ©iStockphoto.com / Joshua Blake

P.25 ©iStockphoto.com
P.26 ©iStockphoto.com / Simon Oxley
P.29 ©iStockphoto.com / Jolande Gerritsen
P.30 ©iStockphoto.com / Jolande Gerritsen
P.39 ©iStockphoto.com / Matt Tilghman
P.41 ©iStockphoto.com / Tulay Over
P.46 ©iStockphoto.com / Jolande Gerritsen
P.53 ©Clipart.com
P.55 ©iStockphoto.com
P.57 ©iStockphoto.com / Justin Welzien
P.59 ©iStockphoto.com / Charity Myers
      ©iStockphoto.com / James Thew
      ©iStockphoto.com / Peter Finnie
P.64 *Hard Frost* by Andrew Young. Extract reprinted by permission of Carcanet Press Ltd.
P.65 *Football At Slack* by Ted Hughes. Extract reprinted by permission of the publisher, Faber and Faber Ltd., London
P.66 © 1937 J R R Tolkien. Reprinted by permission of HarperCollins Publishers Ltd.
P.70 ©iStockphoto.com / Nicholas Monu
P.71 ©iStockphoto.com / Kim Freitas
      ©iStockphoto.com / Martynas Juchnevicius
P.81 Reproduced by permission of OneWorld (http://tiki.oneworld.net)
P.83 ©iStockphoto.com
      ©iStockphoto.com / Kim Bryant
      ©iStockphoto.com / Cruz Puga
P.85 from www.bullying.co.uk. Reprinted by permission of Bullying UK
P.86 ©iStockphoto.com / Joshua Blake

All other images ©2009 Jupiterimages Corporation, and Letts and Lonsdale.